The Talk About "The Nook"

Have you ever asked the question, "Can anything good come out of *'this'*?"... *'This'*—the betrayal. *'This'*—the abuse. *'This'*—the pain; the hurt, the rejection, the abandonment... *'This'* can be any ugliness or darkness that's somehow crept into your life. The answer is an emphatic "Yes!" Yes, there is a light at the end of the tunnel, and yes, there is some goodness that awaits you!

Author Chaundria Zeigler has caused the true events of her life to unfold into the pages of a literary masterpiece that countless people will not only be able to relate to, but learn from.

This is the book that will hit so close to home that readers will wonder, "How did you know my story?" If there is even the mere shadow of darkness lingering in your life, as you delve into the pages of this book, you will be inspired to journey to your place of light.

~ Dr. Kisia L. Coleman,
M.O.D.E.L. (Mentoring Our Daughters, Equipping Ladies)
Ministries, Founder, Kingdom Church International, Co-founder,
Chicago, Illinois

The Nook is a powerful testament of GOD'S undying love and HIS ability to heal, redeem and transform the most broken person, after trauma has devastated their life.

Chaundria's life was ravaged with the unthinkable trauma and in this book, she masterfully draws the reader into her pain, her frustration, her desperation, and her utmost hope for something better; welcoming them to witness her victories, healing, redemption and transformation.

There is power in *The Nook*. There is breakthrough in *The Nook*. There is rejoicing in *The Nook*. And, most important of all, there is healing in *The Nook* for the broken, lost, confused, despondent, uncertain and hopeless, because it carries within its pages the revelation of a place—a nook in GOD'S presence available to all.

The Nook is refreshingly transparent. Chaundria is open and real about the experiences of her life. Her ability to overcome will empower you to press into victory for your own life. And if you're willing, *The Nook* will challenge you to explore a deeper level of forgiveness in your walk with CHRIST as the author did after all she revealed.

I encourage you to get this book. Accept the challenges presented within its pages. And as you are reading, I encourage you to get to the *nook* that is awaiting you in GOD'S presence. Your life will never be the same!

~ Pastor Jamila Jordan Moody,
Author of Before The Throne: The Believers Guide To Authentic Worship For Manifested Miracles And a Transformed Life, Co-founder of Kingdom United International Fellowship, Johnson City, Tennessee

I have just finished reading *The Nook* and all I can say is, "Wow this is an excellent book!" As I began reading it, I found myself being drawn into Chaundria's story. I experienced a wide range of emotions as I read each chapter. From being hurt, as I read the different things that she experienced as a child; to wanting to become her protector and rescuer; and to wanting to be a listening ear. I even began to see some of my own life situations in her story, which opened things up for me to continue working towards my complete wholeness.

THE TALK ABOUT "THE NOOK"

The way Chaundria shares her personal experiences and conversations with God, and the revelation she has received over the years, is wonderful. This story had me crying with her, rejoicing with her and inspired by the way she explains that even though she experienced all that hurt in her life, she doesn't discount it because everything God allowed her to survive, was for her future generations.

One thing that I took away from this book for myself is that the things that I experienced in my life—good, bad or indifferent—can heal, deliver and set others free just by me being open to share my testimony. I can help others realize that they are not alone. God can be everything that they need Him to be, and they can truly be set free from being broken as a result of life experiences. I can inspire them to find the same healing and deliverance that Chaundria and I have found.

I can't wait to purchase the finished product. It is definitely a *must-read*. Thank you for giving me this opportunity!

~ ***Prophetess Tracey E. Armour***,
Owner of Integrity Personified, Steger, Illinois

The Nook

A Place Where I Journey from Darkness to Light

Chaundria Zeigler

The Nook – A Place Where I Journey from Darkness to Light
By Chaundria Zeigler

Publishing Services including cover and interior design, editing, and book coaching by KishKnows, Inc., www.kishknows.com

ISBN 978-0-9990758-0-7
LCCN 2017908735

Some names in this book have been changed to protect the privacy of individuals.

All rights reserved. No part of this book may be reproduced or transmitted in any form or by any means, electronic or mechanical, including photocopying and recording, or by any information storage and retrieval system, without written permission from the publisher, except in the case of brief quotations for the purpose of review or commentary.

Some scripture references are either paraphrased versions or illustrative references of the author. Unless otherwise specified, all other references are from King James Versions of the bible.

Copyright © 2017 by Chaundria Zeigler

Printed in the United States of America

MY PRAYER

Father God,

I thank you for the oil that is on my life
to write this book and silence the enemy.
I pray that every reader will be blessed.
I pray that the oil on every page of this book
will be released to them
for healing and deliverance.
For those called to write,
I pray for an impartation
of this oil
to write their story.

In Jesus' Name,
Amen

DEDICATION

With special thanks to my grandmother Hazel. Thank you for giving to me the greatest gift that you possessed, The Love and knowledge of Jesus Christ. Had it not been for the seed that you planted and your every prayer and supplication poured out before the Father, I would surely be dead by now.

A very special thanks to an incredible group of people who journeyed with me as I walked out my process for purpose: Chauntavia, Chaundivia, Dejahnique, Shawn, Jasmine, Larry Jr, Ean and Chaundranique. I love you all more than words can ever describe.

To my leader, Pastor Ted Howard: Thank you for loving and preaching me back to life; showing me that it is okay to trust who God has placed in my life to shepherd over me. You are truly the epitome of what a leader should be.

To Sophia Ruffin, Thank you. From Periscope to Facebook Live, you have empowered me and have truly been a blessing and a great encouragement to my life, and I thank God for allowing our paths to cross.

A very special thanks to Pastor Kisia and Noleen. From the time I received my first edits, I knew that I was in good hands. I could feel the love, and I thank you both for all your time and excellent editorial suggestions.

CONTENTS

THE TALK ABOUT "THE NOOK" i
MY PRAYER ix
DEDICATION xi

Chapter 1
THE NOOK 1

Chapter 2
BORN TO LOSE, DESTINED TO WIN 9

Chapter 3
THE DEVIL'S PLOT 19

Chapter 4
THE OTHER SIDE 27

Chapter 5
DANCING WITH WOLVES 33

Chapter 6
THE RIPPLE EFFECT 41

Chapter 7
GOD'S PLAN 53

Chapter 8
ADDICTED 61

Chapter 9
MORE THAN A CONQUEROR 69

Chapter 10
BEAUTY FOR ASHES 77

Chapter 11
FROM DARKNESS TO LIGHT 81
CONCLUSION 83
MY CLOSING PRAYER 85
REFERENCES 87
ACKNOWLEDGEMENTS 89
AUTHOR BIO 91
CONTACT INFORMATION 93

Chapter 1

THE NOOK

You keep track of all my sorrows.
You have collected all my tears in your bottle.
You have recorded each one in your book.
Psalm 56:8 (*NLT*)

51 Ada Place is the address that's etched deep within me. It's where I spent a great deal of my life growing up when my mom was away. It was a red house with white trim, and a fence around it with a gate, to keep the dogs, Jet and Dynamite, in the yard. And it was centered between two of the most positively influential men and families in my life.

Next door was Mr. and Mrs. O'Neill, along with their children. Two houses to the right, located on the corner of Ada and Lyth, were Mr. and Mrs. Williams and their daughter. Now neither of these two wives knew it, but their husbands were my "husbands", as in my companions.

I think I've always had an old soul because I can remember days when the other kids were out playing, I would be sitting in my backyard next to the fence, talking to Mr. O'Neill while he tended his garden. When he was not available, I would walk down to the corner and have a seat on the porch with Mr. Williams and chat with him for hours. Sometimes, I would even sit and talk with Mrs. Williams because she was very nice. She would invite me in for a freeze pop or a cold drink while she cooked dinner, and sometimes she would allow me to sit right up under her while she showed me how to knit.

The Nook

I learned many things from these two families. I enjoyed their company and it seemed that they didn't mind having me around all that much either. These families were a haven to me and gave me a sense of stability.

You're probably wondering why a little girl wouldn't spend time with people her own age. Well I did, and I guess this would be a good time to tell you that I was not an only child. I have an older brother, Hunter, and a younger brother, Stan, both from the same mother.

Then there is my baby sister, Lucy, but she didn't come along until I was ten years old. I have another sister, Kim, and a younger brother, Dave, but he came along in my teen years, both on my dad's side, but I didn't see much of them growing up.

I did, however, have a best friend who was my age. She lived right next door to Mr. and Mrs. Williams. We would often play together when she was home. She wasn't allowed to go too far from her home, so I spent more days at her house than she did at mine. Her house was huge. I used to walk in and sit at the piano and play the one song I knew how to play, if you could call it a song. We would play in her bedroom for hours, dressing up our Barbie's. Her older and younger sister would sometimes join us, but for the most part we played alone.

I have to say, that when Mom was away, this was the best place to hang out until she came home. Most of the families in this neighborhood owned their property and everyone looked out for one another. I can even remember getting into trouble and getting a spanking from the neighbors before I could make it home, and get another spanking from my grandmother. For the most part, when Mom was home, she would try to rent an apartment in the neighborhood so that if, or when, she went away again, depending on how long she would be gone, Grandpa could pay the bills and keep the apartment for her until she returned. My grandparents would just go in and gather some clothes for me and my two brothers, and we would come and stay with them.

One of the times that my mother was away was one of the hardest times for me. I believe I was between 7 and 9 years old. At that time, we lived on Riley and I only saw my best friend when I visited my grandparents because I wasn't living near her. However, Mom went away again and I was back staying with my grandparents and could see my friend more often. Not too long, after moving back in with my grandparents, my best friend suffered a severe asthma attack that cut her life short. Just like that, she was gone. Mom was away and Grandma didn't talk about things like this, so I buried it—deep inside. So much that, to this day, I can't even remember her name! I can clearly recall her mother's name and that she had two older siblings that were twins, a boy and girl, that were named after a pair of famous siblings on TV, as well as a younger sister—but her name seems to be a blur. I just buried this loss and hurt deep within me.

The Holy Spirit is still working on this buried grief within me because even as I tell this part of my story, I gasp for air, and tears run down my face.

It wasn't until January of 2017, after reading the first two chapters of Apostle John Eckhardt's book "Destroying the Spirit of Rejection",[1] that I was reminded of this tragedy. I needed a breather, so I put the book down and started watching television. As I was watching, I heard an inner voice say to me *"She died on you."* I saw a picture of her face instantly. She was light skinned—just like me—and she had dark, brown hair. She was my first, and my only best friend. I wept so long and hard that I cried myself to sleep that night. The waterworks started again when I woke up the next morning.

The Nook

Reminiscing back to my childhood, it was right around that time that I started hanging around the house and playing inside my grandmother's small walk-in closet. This closet was just big enough so that I could fully spread out a twin-size blanket from corner to corner. There was standing room inside the closet but I didn't do too much standing because Grandma kept her clothes and coats in there. I'm sure to some there was nothing special about the closet, but for me it was a place of comfort—a place of refuge. A place where a little girl's imagination could run wild. A place where my best friend was right there with me, just as if nothing had ever happened; at least until it was time to step from my nook back to reality.

As a little girl, I would climb into this closet and play for hours and sometimes fall asleep until I heard my grandmother call me to come and eat dinner. I would like to believe that Grandma understood the pain that I was going through, but she just couldn't find the words to explain the loss of my friend.

According to the dictionary, a nook is a recess, a corner or niche, a cranny, a bay, a cavity, or cubbyhole; a hideaway, hiding place, hideout or shelter. For example, "The nook beside the fire." However, when one encounters trauma, the nook can become a place deep within the recesses of the heart. This is what happened to me as time went on.

During this point in my life, I don't really remember going outside much to play with any kids my age. I did, however, continue to visit Mr. O'Neill, and Mr. and Mrs. Williams. I mean how could I not? After all, they were my *"husbands"— laugh out loud*. But seriously, they were the only consistent and stable thing in my life, and if I didn't need anything else I certainly needed consistency and stability.

This time away for my mom was a shorter stay than usual, and I sure was happy to see her when she came home. We left my grandparents' house and moved into the Ferry Grider Projects for a short time, and then moved around the corner on Glenwood. It wasn't Grandma's house, but I was with JoAnn, and that made me really happy. Yes, Mom's name is JoAnn.

I'm not sure why we called her that and I'm not sure if it's true, but I remember hearing that it was because she had my brother and I at such a young age and didn't want to be called Mom. Who cares? Mom, JoAnn—it didn't matter—the woman who had given birth to me was home and we were together.

JoAnn was one of four children, and the only girl born to James and Alberta Houston. My grandmother was a homemaker whose side job was a full-time foster parent. She not only cared for my brothers and me when Mom was away, but she also took in teenage girls from group homes and raised them as her own. Her other "business" was running street numbers on the side. It was like playing the lotto except it was done from the house. Most of the bettors would call, but the ones she knew really well would stop by and give her a list of three randomly selected numbers that they thought would be drawn in the following night's lottery. One of her foster sons would pick up all the money from those who phoned in their bets, and another man would come by and pick up the money, as well as the list of numbers.

How else can I describe my grandmother? Well Grandma Alberta was about five feet and one inch tall. She was light skinned, with thin salt-and-pepper hair that we colored black every other month. Grandma had one good arm and on the other arm was a stump where her hand used to be. I remember asking her one day what happened, and she told me that when she was a little girl, she fell and her hand was run over by a car.

The Nook

To look at her, one could have mistaken this as a weakness, but she was not to be messed with because Grandma could be a firecracker when she needed to be.

Grandma Alberta was kind, but she was not a very affectionate woman. In fact, it was only recently that the Holy Spirit revealed to me one of the times that rejection entered. When I was a little girl, I was very affectionate and I loved to hug. One day, I remember, my grandfather picked me up and dropped me off at Grandma's. I ran into the house, excited to see her. I tried to hug her but she pushed me away and told me to, "Move! It's too hot for all of that." Yeah, Grandma did not do hugs and kisses well.

She also believed in that whole "women are seen and not heard" foolishness. So, when we lived with her, my brothers would be off enjoying their Saturday, while I was stuck cleaning and helping with Sunday dinner. I hated it and was always angry about it! One day, when I was about 12 years old, I remember getting flipped at the mouth. She ran at me and pinned me up against the refrigerator with that stub, balled her good fist up and said, "I will bust you upside your blankety-blanking head if you say another word!" Well, that was certainly the last time I ever gave that little woman some lip! I ran away a few times during my off-and-on stays with her, but I never ever mouthed-off again.

Grandpa James, better known as Fats, was a chunky man that stood about five feet and three inches. He had this great big belly that I would dive into every time I saw him. He was a street man and, yes, a drug dealer. I remember him always being on the go and only stopped at home to eat dinner, drop off groceries or some kind of gift that he had seen and picked up for my brothers and me.

He drove a black Cadillac, and no matter where I was, I could spot that car anywhere. Even when I lived with my mom, if he came by to visit or to drop off money, the minute he blew that horn, I could be across the street playing and would stop everything because "Grandpa James is here", then I would take off running to see him. I loved my grandfather dearly. I think it's because he was more like a father than a grandfather. Grandpa was different than Grandma. He always gave good hugs and sugar (kisses), not to mention he always came bearing gifts. I believe it was because I was the only granddaughter living in Buffalo at the time that Grandpa James spoiled me so much.

My uncle Beanie was the first-born male born to my grandparents. The only things I could remember about him were that he was in the military, he married a Korean woman and settled down in California. He had a stepdaughter named Sunny and a biological daughter named Veronica. One summer, Veronica came to Buffalo for a visit. I remember this well because Mom was not away and because I was the only girl, my grandparents brought me over to keep her company.

I never had the chance to meet my uncle because he never came home for a visit and was murdered when I was a child. I can recall a phone conversation that my mom was having where she repeated the words, "Murder", "Foul play" and "You better not cremate my brother". As a child, I had no clue what any of that meant, the only thing I did understand was that he was dead. This was the second funeral that I had attended as a child and I knew then that I did not like funerals.

My grandparents' second born, Anthony, lived in North Carolina and would come home to visit twice a year. We called him "Frankie", and he was my favorite uncle. He would take time off from work and drive into Buffalo. Uncle Frankie drove a white van with a back-row seat that let out into a bed. It had a mini refrigerator and a sink inside. I'm assuming it was because he had several children that would come with him. I loved it when he came to

The Nook

visit but was always sad when it was time for them to go. I would sometimes hide in the van and try to sneak back to North Carolina with him and his family. I never got away with that plan.

Now last but not least, there was JoAnn and James —fraternal twins. I'm not sure who was born first but she was the outgoing one—the fighter—the aggressive twin of the two. But as you can see, she was the only girl of three boys, had a father who ran the street and a mother who didn't play. My Uncle James, or Uncle Lemmy, as we called him, was laid back; very chill and more passive than aggressive. He was the fun uncle.

None of the kids liked to be around Uncle Lemmy because he had some form of skin cancer that caused his skin to flake and shed all over the place. It smelled bad when he didn't take proper care of it with a special lotion. He loved his Colt 45 beer and always had a forty ounce in his hands. I didn't care so much about the smell of his skin; it was the smell of beer that I never liked.

I loved it when he came around because he would always call me his favorite niece, give me money and make me laugh. And if he was babysitting, we knew that we could do almost anything and we were going to get away with it without getting a beating. As you can see we put the *"dys"* in dysfunctional.

Chapter 2

BORN TO LOSE, DESTINED TO WIN

> My frame was not hidden from you,
> when I was being made in secret,
> intricately woven in the depths of the earth.
> Your eyes saw my unformed substance;
> in your book were written, every one of them,
> the days that were formed for me,
> when as yet there was none of them.
> Psalm 139: 15-16 (ESV)

So, as you read Chapter One, you may have thought, *"This girl's mother is always away, but where is 'away'?"* Well, she wasn't off visiting family nor was she on any type of business trip, and JoAnn was far from being a flight attendant. But as a little girl, I became really good and creative with my lies when people asked, "Where is your mother?"

The truth was, that "away" for my mother was prison. You see, my mother had a problem with keeping her hands off of things that belonged to someone else. That's right, JoAnn was a kleptomaniac. And, it would seem, that the devil had his sights on me from the time I was conceived because a few months after my mother became pregnant with me—she went to jail.

I'm not exactly sure how long of a sentence she was serving. But, in my early twenties, something came up and I needed an original copy of my birth certificate. When I went downtown, the clerk couldn't find anything on file for Buffalo. Confused and up-

The Nook

set, I went and asked my mother about it and she told me to write to Albion New York for my birth certificate. That's right, I was born in prison only to be released to my grandmother while my mother finished serving one of her many prison sentences.

Now, I have to tell you, this information did not sit well with me! I have three other siblings by my mother, so why the heck couldn't one of them be the one born in jail? And what did this mean for my life? Didn't anybody think to send off for a copy of my birth certificate to pass down to me when I grew up? I had so many questions that went unanswered. And so much pain, that I couldn't share with anyone because I was too ashamed. So, I figured, *"I'll just bury it deep within the nook of my heart, just like I have buried every other inconvenient and painful memory of my life."*

Growing up over the years, I remember going into stores with my mother and watching her steal things. Things like meat, clothes, household items, prescription pads from the doctor's office, and sometimes toys for my brothers and me for Christmas.

Now you would think that if you took a child into the store with you while you were stealing, it would be understandable that what you were doing was teaching that child to steal as well—right?

And if that child did steal, it would be okay because, hey, you taught the child that learned behavior—right? WRONG!

When we lived on Glenwood, my mother sent my brother and me to Twin Fair department store to grab something for her. I'm not sure what the toy was but I must have wanted it bad enough, because I stole it. When we got home, I went to my room and was playing with it. However, I forgot to hide it before I fell asleep. Now this woman, who was a thief, somehow knew which toys she had stolen for us. How the heck she remembered, I don't know, but she knew. The next morning, when the store opened, she marched me right back to the store, made me give the toy back and apologize for stealing it. When we got home it was on, she beat my tail every time she thought about me stealing. This must have gone on for a few days. After that, I never stole anything again!

The crazy thing is, even after this incident, she still continued to take me with her when she was out boosting. I didn't understand it until I became older. You know how sometimes memories come to mind and you sit down and really consider them? Well, I realized that as a child, in all the times that I watched my mother steal, she only stole what she could not buy and when she stole things at other times, it was to make money. I remember she had two faithful customers. There was an older Caucasian lady who she always sold the meat to. We would always be there for a while because she and my mother would laugh and talk for hours. When it was time for us to go, my mother would put a few dollars in my pocket.

With the prescription pads, my mother would write out the prescriptions and take it to the pharmacy to get filled. Some she kept for her habit and the rest she took to Jefferson Ave. to an older black lady who would buy the rest of the pills from her. I don't know much about the pill game, but I do remember words like 'uppers, downers, valium and 3's'.

Now judging from this chapter, some might say that my mother was not fit to be a mother, but on the contrary, I feel differently about the matter. At least, I do know that I am older and God has gotten a hold of my heart.

There is something about yielding your heart to Him that will help you understand why He allowed, and continues to allow, certain events to take place in your life. I have often wondered what my life would have been like if I had my mother in it from start to finish. And sometimes I have despised wondering and have asked God, "Why couldn't I have had different parents? Why couldn't I have had this person as my mom? She is such a good mother." We'll talk about Dad later, but I have also asked the same question about my dad.

    The fact of the matter is, everyone has issues and we never know what another person's family secrets are. It wasn't until God started dealing with me, that I started to appreciate the family that I was born into. I now understand that each and every member of my family, on both sides, shaped me to be the person that I am today.

    When I really give thought to it, they really weren't bad, they were all just people trying to be people. So, you see, even though I have had so many reservations in the past about who my family is, I am aware now that it was all in God's plan. And while over the years my mother continued to go back and forth to jail, I learned to make the most of the time that she was home.

    If I can recall correctly, it was between my 20th and 21st birthday that Mom finally reached her breaking point where she decided, and spoke it out loud, "I'm not ever going back to jail!". I believe there was a power in her speaking those words into the atmosphere that caused something to break over her life, because she never went back to jail again.

    When she reached this point, she had her boyfriend of 4 years living with her. To be on the safe side, we'll call him Mr. Man. I saw my mother truly happy for the first time. Heck, I was really happy as well. She was living upstairs and I was living downstairs so I got to see her, if not spend time with her, very often. I'll tell you more about my story during this time, a little later on.

By then I had my first two children. My first born, Chauntavia, was between 4 and 5 years; and my second born, Chaundivia, would have been almost a year old. Mom loved her grandchildren very much and she made it her business to spend as much time with them as possible. Did she give up stealing? No! Remember, I told you, she was a kleptomaniac. I truly believe that this was a *real* disease.

She slowed down a lot with the boosting. She had some kind of crazy sixth sense and she only went out boosting when she had a good feeling. She would only steal brand named clothes for her household and mine, as well as the best quality foods such as lobsters, crab legs, shrimps and the best cuts of beef. She made sure both of our homes were always stocked up with them. Sometimes, if the kids asked for something I couldn't get them, she would go behind my back and get it for them. She never really needed to steal any of these things. However, because she was a kleptomaniac, I believe that it was more of the thrill of the adrenaline rush that fed her addiction to shoplift, that kept her in the stores stealing.

Mr. Man! I loved Mr. Man. He was good to my mother, and even though he couldn't stop her from stealing, he got her clean off the drugs. He was a real working-man and he worked at the Ford Motor Co. Buffalo stamping plant. He had been there well over 10 years when they met, so he was making good money. My mother didn't want for anything and because I was right downstairs from them, neither did I nor my children. He never treated us like stepchildren even when his friends and family came around, he would always introduce us as "my daughter, sons or grand babies". Life was good and I was getting to know my mom. To this day, I thank God for that time that He allowed us to bond.

Yes, everything was great and it was going well, so I'm not sure how crack cocaine slipped into our happy home—but it got them

The Nook

both. Even though they both became addicted, we were all still very close and growing closer every day. Something in me would not allow me to hate my mother, nor hold a grudge towards her. It could have very well been the fact that I had missed her in my life—for all those years—and now that I had her back, I was willing to take her any way I could get her.

I was expecting my third child so I moved into a single family six-bedroom house across town, leaving them in their apartment. I tried not to worry much about what was going on with JoAnn and Mr. Man because I was more focused on staying healthy for the baby. When I was about eight months pregnant, the doctors found a spot on my baby's brain during a routine sonogram. Dejahnique had to be born by C-Section. Two days after her birth, she underwent brain surgery and survived. After Dejahnique was born, I opened up a home daycare and went to school in the evenings to study cosmetology. My mother babysat while I went to school and even though she was happy to have another grandchild, her addiction continued to worsen, so it wasn't too long before she had to move in permanently with me and the kids. Sometimes she would take off for a few days, and return back to us after she had gotten her fix. Then she would rest, hang out with us and then head back out a few weeks later for another fix. She and Mr. Man had split up, but were on and off again. Eventually the addiction became so bad that he lost his job.

Now by this point I had become really good at burying things deep within my heart, so I cannot tell you exactly what year my grandparents passed away. However, I do remember that I was in my mid-20's when my grandfather died in my grandmother's bed. He went into cardiac arrest in his sleep and never woke up. A year and some short months later, Grandma followed him. She slipped into a diabetic coma and never came out, passing away in the middle of the night. There was no will, so my mother moved into their home. She tried to give it to me but I wanted nothing to do with it. This is really where I got to see my mother's heart because she made good use of this three-bedroom single family home. It seemed that every time I turned around, some homeless person was living there. If you needed a meal or someplace warm to sleep, they would say, "Go see Jo—she'll take good care of you."

We still stayed close either by phone or I would just go over and hang out with her. When she moved into Grandma's house, Mr. Man followed. The drugs continued and things got worse. It was right around then that we received the bad news. My sister-in-law called everyone together at her house, my youngest brother and me were the only ones who showed up. She told us, "Your mother was spotted going into the HIV clinic, and she has tested positive." My heart sank into my stomach as I thought, *"No this can't be. I know she has a drug problem but she can get clean again. Things can turn around, she can't leave me now."*

I went back to my grandparents' house and I waited until we were alone, then I asked her. She admitted to it being true. She said, "I should have left him that time that he gave me gonorrhea." I was flabbergasted. It turns out that Mr. Man was sleeping with an old friend of mine who was HIV positive and he had passed the disease on to my mother. I hated him and I wanted him to die, so I was happy when I found out she would never see him again.

I was afraid and hurting so badly. I didn't know what to do because it was almost as if my mother was giving up on life. The drugs increased and she was only half taking care of herself. One of the things that gave me a little comfort was that her twin moved back home to be with her after his relationship had failed. I had no clue what to do and was feeling helpless, I started going to my father's family church, St. James.

This was when I gave my life to Christ. I was about 23 years old at the time. It seemed like every week, I would be crying and

The Nook

asking God to please save my mother. My mother and I never talked about her being sick after that day, and she lived her life as if nothing was wrong. I was determined to make things work. I believed that God would heal her so I did as much as I could to make sure our relationship would continue to strengthen.

After a few months, I left the family church. We were having a three-day revival and there was a visiting pastor who preached a strong word. I had never heard preaching like that, nor had my spirit ever been that stirred. So, following my heart, I went over to Free Spirit and joined his church.

As the years progressed, I grew a little stronger in my faith. I believed in my heart that moving to Free Spirit was a part of God's plan. I believed so strongly that God would heal my mother, especially since my prayer life was growing and I was learning how to pray and ask God for answers. I was hurt as things took a turn for the worse. I had to put my mother into the hospital, but I visited her every day. I would comb her hair and if she was in her right mind, we would talk a little. She even gave her life to Christ and this made me very happy.

I can remember this specific day as if it was yesterday. It was a Thursday, the day before a Good Friday. I went to go see Mom. I greased and braided her hair. She was in-and-out that day, but I asked her, "JoAnn?"
"Huh?"
"Doesn't Stan have a middle name?"
She said, "Yes, it's Carl."
"I knew it! He said that he didn't have a middle name." I exclaimed. We laughed. Then I had to go, so I said, "JoAnn?"
She said, "Huh?"
"I LOVE YOU!", and for the first time in my twenty something years of life, my Mom said, "I LOVE YOU TOO!"
My heart smiled as I turned to walk out the door.

"I'll see you tomorrow Mom."
"OK!"
I was in the house doing hair when I got the call from the hospital. Mom had passed away on Good Friday. I was heartbroken because I wasn't there with her when she passed on. The thought of my mom dying alone while I was doing hair at home made me even more upset. I quit hair school and, after that day, I never did hair again, other than my own and my daughter's hair.

I've heard a saying that goes: "You become like the five people you spend the most time with." I witnessed all of this growing up, yet it seems that God only allowed me to take on the good parts of Alberta, James and JoAnn. When my kids complain about the spankings they got as kids, I tell them about how they would have never survived if JoAnn was their mother, and I describe how my mother would spank me. To this day, I appreciate all those spankings that she gave me because they turned my life in the opposite direction to the path that she took. And even though she never said it until that one special day, I know that it was because she loved me so much, that she chastised me.

Chapter 3

THE DEVIL'S PLOT

The thief cometh not, but for to steal, and to kill, and to destroy: I am come that they might have life, and that they might have it more abundantly.
John 10:10 (KJB)

When we moved from Ferry Grider Projects onto Glenwood, it was one of the longest times that my mother was home from jail. This was a good time in my childhood. I was about 7 years old. I had my mom, and her foster sister, Evelyn, was staying with us. I loved Evelyn because she was nice. I remember, we had a big chalk board and she would play school with my brothers and me. She would even give us real schoolwork. We didn't go over to visit Grandma often but Grandpa always made sure to come and visit us. If I had to pick, I would say that this was the best time of my childhood.

We had been living on Glenwood for a short time when my dad's brother, his wife and four children moved across the street from us. They had two sons that were around my brother Hunter's age, and two daughters around my age. Every day, I would go across the street and play with the girls. We would play for hours until it was time for me to go home. Sometimes, when my mom went across the street with me, they would send all the kids upstairs while they would have adult time. None of us cared because we were having fun.

One of the memories from this period that was deeply suppressed was the very first time I was violated. I was taking part in a play in my early 30's, when a lesbian's aggressive behavior

The Nook

towards me triggered the memory. She kept following me, making passes at me and brushing up against me. One night, I was lying in bed and, like a movie on TV, I started to remember that day when I was first molested.

My mother had taken me and my brother, Stan, around to her friend's house. I had wanted to stay with my uncle and aunt, but they were not home so I had to go. When we got there, my mother sent my brother and me upstairs with the lady's daughter, April, while my mom and her friends had adult time. April was a teenage girl and she was not happy about us having to be in her room. She asked us our names and when we told her, she asked if we wanted to play a game, so we said yes. That's when she locked the door and molested both my brother and me. Neither of us knew any better so we went along with it. When we got home that night, Stan told my mother about the game we had played—my mother was livid. I'm not sure what became of that friendship, but we never visited that house again.

I continued to play with my cousins every day unless I was on punishment. I was always in trouble doing little things that I knew I had no business doing. I didn't know why I was acting out, and neither did my mother.

When my uncle and his wife relocated, we moved too, but we only moved around the corner on Winslow. I was sad that my cousins had moved away, but I had made a new friend that lived a few doors down.

She had this pretty bed that I called the "Pretty Princess" bed. When my grandfather came to visit one day, I asked for one. I was super excited because he didn't just get me the bed—he got me the whole bedroom set. It was a white bed, with a pink and white canopy, a vanity set, and a dresser with a mirror. It was beautiful and I loved it!

THE DEVIL'S PLOT

It was also around this time that my mother started dating my sister's dad. The house on Winslow was strangely designed. We entered through a back door and went up a flight of stairs into the kitchen. The bathroom was off of the kitchen. You walked through the kitchen into the dining room. Off the dining room were two bedrooms. A few steps further from the dining room was the living room. My bedroom was off of the living room.

My aunt, Evelyn, was still living with us, so my mother put up a curtain separating the living room area and the dining room. That was where she and my sister's dad slept. This was a very bad set-up because, coming out of my room early in the morning, I saw things that a young girl should not have seen. Even the kitchen and bathroom setup was bad because I learned what adults did when they sent the kids upstairs or into the next room to play. Not only were they smoking weed, but they had needles and they were putting drugs into themselves and getting high.

I guess Evelyn couldn't take it because she moved out. I really missed her and would cry a lot after she left. One day, she came over and picked up my brothers and me, and took us to see the Harlem Globe Trotters. I was so excited, when I got home that I ran and jumped on the bed where my mother was lying. Then I felt something wet. When I looked down, my mother was lying in a puddle of blood. Evelyn called the ambulance and they rushed her to the hospital. It was something to do with an IUD (Intrauterine device). Evelyn stayed with us until my mother got better. However, she left as soon as my mother did because the adult time in the kitchen started right back up. But this time, it was different. Sometimes my mom would join in the kitchen, and sometimes she didn't. All of a sudden it all stopped for her—she was six months pregnant. I remember her saying that my sister "slid right in" because she never had a sign or symptom of being pregnant.

The Nook

One night, my mom was lying on the couch asleep. My two brothers and I were in the room playing, and my sister's dad, his two brothers and a Caucasian guy were all in the kitchen getting high, when my sister's dad screamed out, "Jo call 911!". Something had gone seriously wrong in the kitchen and his youngest brother was convulsing. I ran into the kitchen and saw the needle hanging out of his arm and his eyes were turning white. I started screaming loudly. I was so terrified. My mother yelled at me to go and sit down, but I couldn't sit down; I needed to know what was wrong with him and why all the adults were screaming his name, telling him to hold on.

From that day on, I was petrified of needles. Every time I went into Dr. McCoy's office, I had to be held down just to get a shot. One day, I fought so hard that the needle broke off in my leg. I was not playing 'get away from me' with that needle! It was not funny then, but it is now, because when I have to go get blood drawn, I still can't look at the needle. Don't tell me what you are doing and don't tell me what I will feel—we can talk about anything except the needle. I start sweating, my breathing gets heavy, I get a bit light-headed and my blood pressure skyrockets. So, when I have to get anything involving a needle, they take my blood pressure at the end of the visit. Yes, I'm 46 years old and still to this day, I do not like needles!

Well, by the grace of God, my sister's uncle lived. However, after that experience, whenever he came over to the house, he didn't sit in the kitchen with the rest of the adults. He sat in the front and watched TV with us. I guess he learned his lesson about having adult time.

While my mother was in the hospital having the baby, Aunt Evelyn came over to the house to look after us. I'm not sure what was going on but we never went to Grandma's house, and Grandpa didn't visit all that often. I was excited when my mom brought my new baby sister home from the hospital. We were exactly ten years apart, and I was a proud, doting, big sister. Her name was Lucy, but I called her Pebbles. I always had her with me; she was like my real-life baby doll. Of course, the adults went back to the kitchen and my mom joined them, but I kept an eye on Pebbles while they did their thing.

One day, my mother went out somewhere and she asked me to keep the baby. She was gone so long and I wanted to go out and play with my friend, so I wrapped my baby sister up and took her with me down the street, to my best friend's house. When my mom and my sister's dad returned, she came looking for me and of course, beat my behind. But that wasn't the end of it for me. I was really feeling brave because I told her it wasn't her baby—she was my baby! My sister's dad had to stop her from killing me. He got me dressed and took me to his mother, Big Lucy. I stayed at her house for a few days and I hung out with his niece. His niece had an older brother, Eddie, and we all had something in common—Mom problems—their mother had run off and left them.

Now, maybe my sister's dad didn't know that Eddie had some issues, because if he did, I'm sure he would not have left me there. It felt like déjà vu. The only difference was that it was a boy this time—his nephew molested both me and his sister that night when Big Lucy had gone to church. I never told my mother, it was just another thing that I buried deep within. Whenever my mother tried to take me to Big Lucy's house, I screamed and cried, and eventually she never took me there again.

One day, my mom wanted to go to bingo and she was going to take us over to Big Lucy's house, but I snuck down to my friend's house and called my grandfather. I asked him to come and get me, and he did.

The Nook

   Now, back then there was a serial killer on the loose named Joseph G. Christopher—better known as the "22-Caliber Killer". He had murdered 12 individuals and wounded numerous others, with almost all being African Americans. Well, after my mother returned from bingo, she and my sister's dad, and his brother, were all at the house in the kitchen getting high. The 22-Caliber Killer fired 4 bullets into our apartment and drove off. Two bullets were found in our living room wall, while two were found in my bedroom wall when the police arrived to investigate. I remember hearing my mother say that she was happy that she allowed us to go to our grandparents' house.

   Shortly after this, she started looking for a house and I remember that she wanted a place near my grandparents. This must have made my sister's father very upset because one day they started arguing about it, and as we were getting out of the car, he got out and they started tussling. My heart was racing and I was terrified. I ran into the house, grabbed a knife and ran back down the stairs and tried to stab him. My mother screamed, "Oh my God!" She grabbed my hand and took the knife, he ran and got in the car and my mother yelled at me to get in the house. I wanted out; I couldn't take it anymore. I was not used to all this mess that I had faced at her house, and I wanted to go back to my grandparents' home.

   My mother found a house around the corner from my grandparents on Alexander Street, and even though I lived with her, I stayed with my grandparents most nights. A little while after we had moved, my mother discovered why my sister's father didn't want us moving on Alexander. He had been seeing another woman, and had a son and daughter by her.

   What's really ironic is that they lived right next door in the upper apartment at 99 Alexander, and we were moving into the lower apartment, under her sister, at 101 Alexander. Needless to say, they broke up. My mom and the lady actually became close friends.

   I believe we were living there a little over a year before Mom went back to jail. My brothers and I moved back in with my grandparents—I was almost fourteen when she came home.

Chapter 4

THE OTHER SIDE

"He will restore the hearts of the fathers to their children and the hearts of the children to their fathers, so that I will not come and smite the land with a curse."
Mal 4:6 (NASB)

My father, Henry Zeigler, was one of 7 boys and 4 girls—a total of eleven children—born to my grandparents, Hazel Grady and Henry Zeigler Sr. There is not very much that I can tell you about my grandfather, for most of my life I thought he was dead. No one ever mentioned his name or talked about him.

And then, one day when I was in my mid to late 20's, I got a call from my sister-in-law who was working at the nursing home. She asked me what I was doing and when I told her I wasn't doing anything, she insisted that I come to the nursing home to see a man that looked just like me. My car was not working, so I called my sister, Kim, to take me to see this man. As soon as we walked onto the 2nd floor of the nursing home, we instantly knew that an older gentleman who walked past us, was the man she was talking about. He looked like our father's identical twin, except he was very pale in complexion and had blue eyes. We told him who we were and walked back to his room to visit and talk with him. He had previously lived in Alabama and had made his way to Buffalo to see my dad and the rest of his children by my grandmother, but everyone declined the visit except my Aunt Barb.

We stayed and visited for a little over an hour and told him we would be back, but before we could visit again, his other children came to take him back to Alabama. I never got a chance to see him again; he passed away a few years ago.

When I asked my uncle about it, he said that my grandfather was abusive. When he and Grandma split up, she moved away from him and remarried.

Grandma Hazel was a godly woman. If she wasn't sitting on the porch surrounded by her children, you could find her at church. It was Grandma Hazel who introduced me to God. I only got to visit my father's side when my mom was home from jail, and then later in my teen years, I would walk over and visit them on my own. Any time that I stayed the weekend at her house, she would make sure that before I returned home, I attended the Sunday Service at our family church.

My dad—I remember my dad always had something going on. Every time I went to see him, for the most part, I ended up being upstairs with my grandmother and my aunt that was my age, because Dad either had company or he was cleaning, or he was heading out. Yup, my Daddy was a busy man. When I was a little girl, I didn't mind him not spending much time with me because I enjoyed hanging out with my aunt. Come to think of it, he was always "busy" when it came to me.

What makes me say that? Well, one of my dad's sisters was close friends with my mom, so my mother always found out when my little sister Kim, from another mother, was visiting my dad. Mom would be on the phone, and suddenly she would start cussing and fussing, followed by, "And he's going to watch mine too!" Next thing I knew, she was shoving money into my tights and pushing me into a cab with instructions, "And you better not take that money out until you get in the house to give it to an adult!" Now, this was not the only time she would do this because some days, it was random. I'm not sure if you've figured it out by now, but my mother was not a force to be reckoned with. At any given time, you could find a hammer, a hatchet or a knife in her purse—and I've heard conversations of her pouring things like lye, bleach and hot grits on people. I can't say for sure, but if I had to guess, I would say that my dad had encountered her side of crazy before, so when I showed up at the door, no matter what time of night it was, he would let me in and take me upstairs.

My dad and I never had a close relationship. Even as a little girl, I can remember many days sitting on the radiator and looking out the window, waiting for my dad to come and fetch me like he said he would—but it never happened. At the age of thirteen I was allowed to walk around the three blocks to my father's house, but to no avail—we still never connected. At the end of that summer, just after I had turned thirteen, Grandma Hazel announced her plans to move back to Alabama. I desperately wanted to go with her, but my mother was still in jail and Grandma Alberta didn't want us around my father's family, so I knew her giving me permission to go was not going to happen.

When I was 14 years old, I started becoming rebellious towards Grandma Alberta, and I was fed up with always having to keep an eye on my baby sister Lucy. The only time I didn't have to watch her was when my grandmother allowed me to go skating, which I tried to do every weekend so that I could get out of that house—plus, I was tired of doing all of the housework and I wanted out. It didn't help at all that my grandfather had moved out—I blamed her that he was gone. At any rate, I just didn't want to be there anymore. I asked my dad if I could please come and live with him, and he sat me down then gave me all these ridiculous rules: I couldn't go outside if he wasn't home, I couldn't have company, I had to help with the cooking and cleaning—and he never ever wanted to see me sitting on my favorite Uncle Tom's lap ever again. Well, there was no way I was leaving one prison to move into another, so I stayed with Grandmother Alberta.

The Nook

Over the years, my dad and I had some failed attempts at building a relationship. Once, when I was in my early 30's, I remember my brother Hunter getting all of my dad's children together for a family dinner. For the first time, I thought that this was it and that we would finally hit it off. And we did—we laughed and talked and had such a good time that my brother said, "Okay, next month we'll do this at Mooch's house." Mooch is my nickname that both sides of my family called me. Dad and his wife agreed, and I was excited. I went home and started planning out the menu. I was doing it up big because my big brother had offered to pay for everything. All I had to do was draw up the shopping list and he would buy everything.

With just three weeks to go before the big family dinner, my phone rang and it was Dad, "Hey baby. How are you?"

"I'm good and you?"

"Not so good. That's what I'm calling about. I have to cancel our plans I have a bad nosebleed and I won't be able to make it." My heart sank. I looked at the phone, then put it back to my ear; "Okay Dad. Well let me know if you change your mind because it's still three weeks away." I hung up the phone and called my brother. I told my brother what happened and then said in the sternest voice, "Don't you ever ask me to try to fix this thing again with your Dad because I am done!" I hung up the phone, went up to my bedroom and cried.

I was depressed for weeks. I couldn't understand why Dad loved Hunter, Kim and Dave more than he loved me. What was wrong with me? Why didn't he love me? Finally, the man I was living with at the time had had enough. My two daughters and my son were still at home. He asked me, "Are you just going to lie there and die? What about your children?" I knew he was right, so I got up and got myself together. At this point I was growing serious about my walk with God, so I started studying more and praying more. I did everything I could to not focus on that pain—I guess you can say, I buried it...

Dad and I didn't talk much after that. I often prayed that God would mend our relationship before we got old and one of us died. The only time I saw him was if the both of us were at a family functions, we would speak, but for the most part, I kept my distance.

Then one day, in 2014, I got a phone call saying that I needed to get up to Roswell Park Cancer Institute, and say goodbye to Dad. It was late when I arrived and everyone was gone, but because I had my badge and some of the staff knew me, they let me into the room. He was unresponsive and so I began to talk to God and asked Him for time. I told God that my dad couldn't die like that; we had to make amends before he died. The next day, Dad was awake and talking. One of the best parts about him being in Roswell Park was that I was working in medical records and I could walk over on my breaks and lunch to visit him. Dad was in the hospital for a few weeks, and I had very understanding supervisors, so every day I would go over and sit with Dad while his wife was at work. I remember one day walking up the hall to visit him and as he spotted me he started smiling. I could read his lips as he said to my cousin "Mooch". I smiled too because it felt good to see that he was happy to see me. During our visits we laughed, we talked and we bonded, and God gave me what I needed most—closure.

Dad died in October of 2014, but before he passed, I found out things like my flat, fat feet looked just like his. We both had a gift to write poetry. He could write his on a whim; and once upon a time, a long, long time ago, Daddy was a preacher and he walked away from the calling. It wasn't easy saying goodbye to Dad but I am truly grateful to God for allowing me the time to get things right before he left us.

Chapter 5

DANCING WITH WOLVES

> Save me, O God,
> For the waters have threatened my life.
> I have sunk in deep mire, and there is no foothold;
> I have come into deep waters,
> And a flood overflows me.
> Psalm 69:1-2 (*NSV*)

My grandmother had a sister, Aunt Florence, who was a hairdresser. From time to time, she would come by and pick my brothers and me up to go hang out at her house. Other times she would just pick me up to come and help her clean up, so that I could make some extra money. Now, when I was a young girl, I loved to dance. I would even sing and dance while I cleaned up. Aunt Florence never minded funding something, as long as we were being productive. At the time, I was about 12 and a half years old, she told me that she was going to ask my grandmother if she could put me in jazz class. I was excited when Grandma said yes!

Dance was hard work, but I loved it because I was doing something that I enjoyed doing. I made sure all of my homework was done, even if I had to stay up late on the two days that I had danced. On the weekends, I went to Aunt Florence's house to do chores. This was certainly a time that I didn't mind cleaning.

We didn't attend church at Grandma Alberta's house—I didn't know it back then, but Grandma was a Catholic. She had statues of Jesus and Mary that I played with as a little girl, and I often saw her reading a card while she held a cross with beads on it.

The Nook

This did not appeal to me at all, so some Saturdays, I spent the night with Aunt Florence. Her two children were grown and off to college so it would just be Aunt Florence, Uncle Ozzie and me in that great, big house. It was quiet and peaceful, and it was a nice change of pace not having to babysit Lucy.

I had been in dance class for almost a year when JoAnne came home from jail. The timing could not have been better. You see, the people across the street from my grandmother's house had just moved out and the house was for rent. I was happy because I wouldn't have to move away, and I could still take my dance classes. The house was huge and we only had a little bit of furniture, so I had plenty of space to move and practice. My brothers and I all lived with my mother, but they were always across the street at my grandmother's house. My mother lived at bingo when she wasn't with her new boyfriend Dean, so I was often home alone after school and dance class. I would grab something to eat and then practice a little bit before heading to bed.

By this time, I was a fully developed, young lady. I hated my shape because it drew the attention of boys and men all ages. I liked baggy clothes because they hid my figure. Before JoAnn came home, Grandma gave me money and let me get on the bus to go shopping for my own clothes.

I always made sure to be with a friend or cousin when I wasn't near home because I was paranoid of being touched again. However, JoAnn didn't make this easy for me because she thought I had a cute shape and so she would pick me up clothes that would show off my figure.

One day, she took me out boosting with her and her boyfriend, Dean, who drove a taxi. Now, I have to admit, this man was cute. He had dark brown skin, pretty white teeth, and had those big brown eyes. His hair was like nothing I had ever seen on a Black person before. He had long, black silky hair that he wore loose. I thought, "This man was very handsome!", but I never said what I was thinking out loud. That day, we stopped back at the house, and JoAnn ran into Grandma's house to drop off the stolen goods. She left me in the car with Dean. He and I were talking and before I knew it, he had his hand on my thigh, rubbing me. I clenched up and started trembling, so he told me I was safe and that he would never hurt me. He whispered, "I would never do anything to you that you wouldn't want me to do." Right there, in broad daylight, he leaned over the seat and kissed me near my lips. A tear ran down my face and I kept looking for my mother to come back outside. She was taking so long that I jumped out of the cab and ran into the house. When she was ready to go, I told her I was tired and wanted to stay home. They drove off and I went into my grandmother's house and got into the bed with her.

When she asked me what was wrong, I told her I was just really tired and didn't feel well. That day, my grandmother's dog, Dynamite, came to the side of the bed where I was lying. He put his face on the bed and stayed there while I slept.

After that day, I did everything that I could to avoid Dean. If he came to the house, I went across to Grandma's house, and if JoAnn announced that she was going to his house or we were going somewhere with him, I disappeared until they had left.

THE WOLVES

That summer, when I was 14, Grandma Hazel came back to Buffalo for an extended visit and she had brought her godson, John, with her. I'm not exactly sure why or how, but he ended up staying with us during their visit. My mother gave him her room. I was still taking my dance classes, but since my grandmother was in Buffalo, all of her kids and their kids gathered at her house on Waverly. I was allowed to stay over late because

The Nook

John was there and I could walk home with him when it was time to go.

One night, after my dance class, I decided that I would stay home. I was exhausted from all the late nights and just wanted to sleep. My mother was at bingo and my brothers were across the road at Grandma Alberta's house or were outside playing, so as soon as I got into the house, I took a shower put some pajamas on and lay down. I'm not sure how long I was asleep, but I must have been in a really deep sleep because I didn't hear anyone come into the house—nor did I hear John come into my room. I woke up and he was on top of me with his shirt off and his pants unbuttoned! He had pulled the shirt of my pajamas up, and was trying to pull my pajama bottoms off. I grabbed my pants with one hand and started fighting with the other—and tried to push him off me. It seemed that the more I fought, the stronger he got! I couldn't do anything but scream because the scratching and the biting didn't stop him, and he almost had my bottoms off. I had been touched and I had been fondled, but nothing like this had ever happened; I was about to be raped in my own house— where I was supposed to be safe.

Just then I whispered in my head, *"JESUS PLEASE!"* Suddenly, there was a loud crash and laughter. My two brothers came into the house and were running around downstairs. John jumped up, got dressed and ran out of the house. I sat up, but I couldn't move because I was trembling so hard and crying.

So many thoughts were racing through my mind, *"Why does this keep happening? Was it my fault? And where the heck was this God that Grandma Hazel said was so good? I'm going to tell my uncle so that he can kill him!"* And I knew if I did tell any of my uncles, this boy would come up missing for real. My uncles were good men, but they were violent— committing murder was not beneath them.

When I finally pulled myself together, I got dressed, then went across the street and hid in my Nook—the closet in my grandma's room. I decided to stay there until my mother came home from bingo. I had had enough. This was not going to happen to me anymore. Today is the day I would tell someone. My mother was gone for so long that I fell asleep.

It was evening when I woke up and went back home. When I got in the house, JoAnn had company; her friend Krystle, 'the rock lady.' Now I couldn't put my finger on it, but something just wasn't right about this lady. Krystle had to be every bit of six feet tall and she was a heavy woman with a deep voice. I steered clear of this lady because she freaked me out badly. Every time she came around, I had a horrible feeling in the pit of my stomach.

I called her 'the rock lady' because she was into this crazy stuff where she would pour rocks onto the table and tell people private stuff about their lives. She also had these funny colored rocks that she passed out, depending on what was wrong with you. Whenever we went to her house, I stayed in the hallway or on the porch. She was always touching my cheek and telling me about something called an aura.

So, that night, I was not happy to see her at all. There was another woman there too, that I didn't know, and Dean. They were all drinking and partying, so I asked my mom if I could talk to her. She got up and followed me into the kitchen where I told her everything. I told her about the girl April, which she already knew about because my brother had told her. I told her about my sister's cousin Eddie, and what he did to his sister and me the night I was left at Big Lucy's house. I told her about her boyfriend Dean, and also about my grandmother's godson, John, almost raping me that afternoon. She didn't believe me—my mother didn't believe me!

The Nook

I became so angry and enraged that I flipped out and started cussing my mother out. I told her she didn't believe me because she must have been sleeping with this young dude. I tried to tell her that the reason I got out of the cab, a few months back, was because of what Dean did to me. And that's when she slapped me so hard that I fell on the floor. Her friend, Krystle, jumped up and stood in between us. While she was blocking my mother, I jumped up, ran out the door and around to my Uncle Tom's house.

I told him everything that had happened. Uncle Tom was a huge man, almost 6 feet tall and was very stocky. So when he told me I could lie down in his room and that everything would be okay—I believed him. I went into his room. At first I sat there thinking about all that had happened, and wondered why all this was happening to me. I must have dozed off because when I woke up, it was a little past 1 am and the police were knocking at the door looking for me.

Uncle Tom lived over some type of storefront that had been closed for years. When you went up the front stairs, you could get into his apartment from the front hallway. When you went out the back door, there was an apartment in the back that only had one way in and one way out. One of Uncle Tom's friends lived in that back apartment, so my uncle told him to let me into his apartment to hide. I remember thinking, "Great—she's called the cops on me. Now I can never go home." Uncle Tom had been arrested several times before, so he knew the police officers, and he let them into his apartment. He told them that he and the boys had been there all night, drinking and playing cards and they never saw me. After the cops left, so did all his company; there's just something about the cops coming around that can mess up a good time. I came back across the hall and went back into my uncle's room.

Shortly afterwards, he came in and started talking to me. "Have you ever had sex before?"
"No never."
"Have you ever let a man kiss you in the mouth?"
"No!"

Then he started explaining what happens when you have sex, and what will happen when a man penetrates you. As he walked towards me, I started getting really uncomfortable. He put his hand on my shoulder and told me to relax, and that he wasn't going to hurt me. He kissed me on my cheek and told me to lie back—I wanted to die. I wished he would just kill me right then and there, because this was just not happening to me! As I lay there, he pulled my pants off and started performing oral sex on me. I tried not to breathe or make a sound; tears were running down the sides of my face. "Why doesn't he just kill me? Just let him kill me God!" Suddenly he stopped, told me to pull my pants up and went into the bathroom. I fixed my clothes and sat on the bed, with tears still streaming down my face. I trusted him, he was my uncle and I ran to him for safety. Why would he do this to me? I remembered the conversation with my Dad when he told me he never wanted to see me sitting on Uncle Tom's lap again. Did he know that this was what this man did? Was that his way of protecting me and if it was, why didn't he do a better job?

When Uncle Tom came out of the bathroom, he told me to lie down and get some sleep. He wasn't going to do anything. I lay on the other side of the bed against the wall, wide awake all night, while he slept on the edge of the bed.

The next morning, he took me across town to a Caucasian woman's house. He told me that he would come back for me when things cooled down, and that I could take the time to get to know his daughter, who was a year older than me. Before he left, he gave the mother some money and pulled me aside. He warned

The Nook

me not to say anything. I was there for about two weeks before I called my mother and asked her if I could please come home. I had to get out of there—the mother was about four sides of crazy and she had passed two of those sides off to her daughter!

Mom told me that she would meet me at Masten Park, where the daughter was working in the Mayor's Summer Youth program. So, that day I went to work with the daughter. I was so happy to see my mother. When she walked into the park, I hugged her and cried; then we got into her friend's car, and she took me straight to the hospital. While we were at the doctors, she asked me if my uncle had touched me. I wanted to say yes, but all that I could remember was her calling me a liar—so I said no. After we left the doctor's office, as soon as we got home, I went across to my grandmother's house, got into her bed and slept for a few days. When my aunt called to inquire about my dance classes, I told my grandmother that I wasn't going anymore, I didn't feel like dancing. I had gone from a little girl who had a passion for the art of dance, to a girl who wanted nothing to do with it.

Chapter 6

THE RIPPLE EFFECT

He brought me up out of the pit of destruction,
out of the miry clay,
And He set my feet upon a rock
making my footsteps firm.
Psalm 40:2 (*NASV*)

Well wouldn't you know it! Just when a girl needs her mother, she goes back to jail, and as if that wasn't enough— Grandpa James was arrested on drug possession. The devil was trying to kill me for real, and I had no weapons to fight back. Grandma Alberta was a Catholic praying to some beads, and Grandma Hazel had returned back home to Alabama.

Now if all of that wasn't enough, I had the nerve to be going crazy—or so I thought. A few years back, someone had left the door open at Grandma Hazel's house and the dog ran outside and was hit by a car. Not too long after that, I started having visions of a little girl lying in the street, dead. I would come outside, lay my hands on her, and she would get up. I didn't get these visions often but when I did, I would try to think of something else... anything else. Well, after all of the trauma, the visions increased and I would see them at least once a week. I didn't tell anyone because I thought I was going nuts, and the last thing I needed was for them to put me away in the loony-bin. I had no clue of what was going on and I didn't have nearly enough church in me to battle through it, so I retreated even deeper—within the nook of my heart.

The Nook

   I was ashamed and fearful to tell anyone that I had been molested several times. This was because I never wanted to be judged or give anyone else the opportunity to say that the molestations were not true. So, I buried it all deep within me and my hurt manifested outwardly in other ways. By the time I had turned 15, my behavior became horrific. I put away all the girly stuff and started doing things such as playing football and wrestling with the boys. I even started to get into fights—often. If I saw someone bullying another kid, I jumped in and beat the bully up. If someone was bothering one of my siblings, I beat them up. I remember smashing a boy named Sean's head into the tires of a car repeatedly because he was bothering my brother. This was who I had become, and if I was having a bad day and you got in my way, the fight was on. I didn't care if it was a boy or girl, big or small; I was not allowing anyone else to mess with me or anyone that was around me. The problem was, all that fighting got me kicked out of school. This happened at every school and eventually there was no other school for me to go to other than the Alternative. So, I finished the rest of grammar school at Buffalo Alternative.

   School was not the only place that I acted out. I had two brothers that I lived with and they were holy terrors at times, at least they were before I started attacking back. My baby sister Lucy never got on my bad side, so she was always safe. Now, do you remember I told you that my grandfather would bring us gifts? Well, he brought frilly little girl things for me, like dolls, dresses and hair bows. But for the boys, he brought home snakes, big huge hairy spiders and bugs. My brothers thought that it was cool to torture me with their pets. But, when I changed the game, it was no more miss nice sister! All it took was one act of violence, and they never bothered me again. One day, I was watching TV in my grandmother's room when Hunter came in and changed the channel. He fell asleep on the floor at the foot of my grandmother's bed. There was a tall dresser near his head and on the dresser, was a thick glass statue of a lady.

I purposely knocked it over and it broke, and gashed my brother's eyebrow open. There was so much blood! I was terrified that my grandmother was going to kill me because out of the 4 of us, Hunter was her favorite, but surprisingly she didn't. She just yelled at me and sent me to my room.

A few weeks later, I was in my room watching TV and Stan wouldn't stop bothering me. He kept throwing my Uncle Lemmy's platform shoes into my room. I waited until he peeked his head around the banister and I clobbered him right in the head with the shoe—again blood everywhere. This time I didn't even worry about the repercussions. I told my grandmother it was a mistake, closed my bedroom door and locked it so I didn't have to hear her cussing and fussing. Even though they left me alone, I went at them all the time. I would go into my brother's room and sneak his clothes. If they were watching scary movies, I would hide under the dining room table and wait until they walked by; then grab their legs and scare the mess out of them. The old me was gone and the new me was, as my brother Hunter once described it, "as mean as a rattle snake". I had moved from passive to passive aggressive.

I had become a bit of a tomboy, so I had male friends calling at the house for me. At that time, I wasn't interested in boys but for whatever reason, every time a boy called, my grandmother felt the need to tell me how I had "better not come up in her house with no baby." I wasn't even having sex, but I was so tired of her saying that mess, that I set out to have sex just to spite her.

Some weeks after that, I met my first boyfriend and even though I wanted to, I was too afraid to have sex. Eventually we broke up. This just caused me to harden my heart even more. Eventually, I met my daughter's father and we hit it off. I didn't know it at the time but heck, he was just as broken as me. JB was persistent; and finally, I gave in. Then I ended up pregnant at the age of 15.

The Nook

My mother was released from jail when I was about 6 weeks pregnant, and it didn't take her long to figure out that I was carrying a child. She took me straight to the abortion clinic. Laws were not like they are now and I had to get the abortion—she killed my baby and I hated her! I continued to live with my grandmother, but my two brothers and Lucy went to live with my mother across town. My mother was so wrapped up with Mr. Man that she didn't come around often, so JB and I were at it again and in a few months I was pregnant again. This time, my mother violated her parole and had to go back to jail for ninety days. By the time she got out, I was too far gone for her to make me get an abortion. After my daughter was born, JB and I were fooling around and for the first time I was stimulated. From that moment on, if we weren't fighting, we were fooling around.

My grandmother had had enough of us fighting, and breaking things in her house. She told me that I needed to move in with my mom. I wanted nothing to do with my mother at the time because of the abortion, so I went down town and emancipated myself. I got a one bedroom apartment on the other side of town, and a friend of my mother watched my daughter when I went to school.

JB and I had broken up and I started seeing someone else. My landlord was an older lady, so every time I had company, she wanted to know who was up there. At the time, I had a friend staying with me so of course this was more trouble—both of our boyfriends coming by all hours of the night. This lady was tripping! One day, I came home from school and Nique was gone, but the landlord was in my apartment stripping and waxing my floors. I started looking for an apartment the next day!

My mother called and told me that the apartment downstairs from her was for rent, and I figured that my daughter could stay at home more and school was right down the street. So, I moved downstairs from my mother. I was going to school and most days

THE RIPPLE EFFECT

Nique watched my daughter. When she couldn't, my mother and Mr. Man watched her. And, as I mentioned before, this was the season when my mother and I started getting close again.

Now, I was the only girl in school with my own apartment, so my house became the 'skip school party house'. I had a cousin who lived with his grandmother two doors down from me, so some days I would be at school and my cousins would be at my house having a 'skip school party.' It was wild! I would come home from school and my house would be packed.

It was also around this time that I met baby number two's daddy, ER. My friend Nique was pregnant, and had moved in with her boyfriend. I was fine with it because I had my mind on other things, like ER. This boy was FINE! A bad-boy. The day that we met, the thing that caught my attention was one of his eyes. It was an all-night skate party and I had skated for hours and was tired. I happened to be looking in his direction and this one eye kind of shined. It was later that night that I noticed this one pupil was round and the other, the one that shined, was oval—like a cat's. I didn't know why then, but I had to get to know him. So I went over, sat next to him and pretended to be cold until he gave me his coat. I sat next to him for the rest of the night talking and when the skating was over, I put my phone number into his pocket.

The next day, he called me and I invited him over. So I ditched 'what's his name' and started fooling around with ER. Eventually he moved in with me and my daughter, and it wasn't long before I was pregnant again. I was so in love with this man that, of course, there wasn't nothing that he could do wrong. However, that all changed within a day. I was ten days overdue and was on my way home from seeing the doctor, I looked out the window of the train, and saw him with another girl. I was crushed. By the time I made it home, I was so upset that I went into labor.

The Nook

My cousin T-love and I were very close. He had been around every day of the pregnancy and he also had a baby due in about two months by Teres. T volunteered to go into the labor room with me. I didn't want to be alone, so I said yes. He rode to the hospital with me and held my hand while I gave birth to my second daughter. ER was fine-looking, but that was it for me. I wanted nothing else to do with him, but I knew I had to have a roughneck because ER was a fighter and there was no way he was just going to let me go. So, I hooked up with Tone. His crew was large, so I knew I would be okay.

I was becoming more and more reckless by the minute. My cousin T-love introduced me to the girls that he hung out with and they introduced me to MD 20/20 with flavors. I started drinking and partying every weekend, and on occasions smoking marijuana. If I wasn't at the club, then I was at home having a co-ed pajama party. The girls who I hung out with at school, would have their moms call my mom and ask if it was okay for them to stay. And some of the boys' parents were under the impression that the boys were spending the night with my brothers. Little did they know that we would all be in the same apartment drinking, partying and some were fornicating. Tone and his friends would always be at these parties, just so there was no misunderstanding that I was available. I partied so much that I failed two classes in my senior year, and had to finish my high school years with summer school—but even that didn't stop the partying.

What happened to Tone? Linda happened to Tone. I threw him a birthday party. That night he had given me his pager to hold and when she messaged him, I called her back and invited her to the party. And to get rid of Tone, there was Bill—my third daughter's father.

When I met Bill, I had been single for almost 6 months on purpose. I just needed a break from men. I had been working at a nursing home for over a year, when he was hired. I was beginning to realize that I needed to be a better mother for my girls and things were starting to turn for the better. I still drank and partied but not as much. I was starting to slow down, and get my head on straight. The staff at the nursing home put us together to lift and assist heavy patients, and we hit it off. Before we knew it, we were a couple. This didn't sit right with the head nurse because she, and several other girls, wanted to be with him. One day, the head nurse and one of the other aides lied about me, and I was fired.

It was a few months before Christmas, and I was back on the road to destruction. I took to the streets and started hustling crack cocaine. Neither Bill nor my mother wanted me getting caught with the drugs, but Bill had his own to sell, so I didn't want him selling mine plus I needed to make my own money. I was independent like that. So, we came up with a system. By this time, my daughter's dad, ER, had become big time in the drug game so I hooked up with him to purchase the drugs and my mother sold them. She would call me when it was time to collect the money from her and call ER so that I could re-up.

I was so stubborn that I didn't even want to use Bill's contacts. I had to use my own. After I got all my kids their Christmas toys, I continued to hustle for about eight months, but I had to stop because I didn't like who I was becoming. I remember going to pick up the money from my mother and I heard her scream my name as I drove past. I stopped, backed the car up and when I got out she was cursing a girl out for continuously bullying my sister. The car was still rolling when I jumped out and I ran full force at the girl, and jumped up into the air kicking her in the face with the free leg. I had combat boots on at the time and blood was everywhere, that didn't stop me because I jumped on top of her and started punching her. My mother was screaming "Mooch please STOP!". Something snapped inside of me and I came to my sens-

The Nook

es. I don't know what had gotten into me—this girl's mother used to braid my hair when my mother was in jail.

Less than 2 weeks later my mother's friend, Sally, stopped by to get a product on credit. I said it was fine because she was good for it. The next day, when I went to collect the money, she said she didn't have it and they had smoked all of my product—so I jumped on her. Now I was raised to never disrespect my elders, so that night I was sick to my stomach at what I had done. I cried all night asking God what was wrong with me. Who was this ugly person? Bill told me that I wasn't cut out to be a hustler and I needed to get out of the game, so I agreed.

I had to swallow my pride and go file for public assistance to help with bills until I could find a job. However, before I could find something, I ended up pregnant with Dejahnique. Bill and I stayed together for a few months after I had my daughter. I was on bedrest pretty much the whole pregnancy. A few weeks after I had my daughter, I found out that while I was pregnant, Bill was leaving me in the house alone and was spending time with Tiny. Tiny was pregnant and due around the same time as me. However, it wasn't his baby. It didn't matter to me that it wasn't his baby but what hurt me the most was that I was carrying his child and he left me alone to be with another pregnant woman. As she and I talked, she was kind, respectful and honest, and she even tried to console me; but I was so broken, that my loyalty for this guy was out the window.

And so, to get rid of Bill, I hooked up with my son's father, Seth. My life was continually going in a downward spiral. With each relationship, I lost a huge piece of who I was. However, to end one relationship it always took someone tougher than the last one—just to get free. I had other relationships between some of these, but they were short term. Some left scars in my heart. And because I was wounded, with the others, I left unintentional scars in their hearts. I guess it's true what they say, "Hurting people hurt people." So, I needed to be healed from the *'one abusive relationship after another syndrome.'*

In my heart, I believed that if I could just find one person in this world that would love me the way I needed to be loved, everything would be fine. I was searching for something that was missing, but what I needed was not in any of those men nor in the fulfillment of lust that they provided. What my soul was crying out for was healing! And my spirit was screaming to be made whole again. I was just unaware that there was One who would love me unconditionally.

I had dated my son's father, Seth, off and on for sixteen years. I served prison terms with him. By that I mean that while we were together, when he went to jail, I visited, sent packages and money. After fifteen years of this, we were planning to get married when he came home. However, I ended up getting pregnant and giving birth to my son, Shawn.

To cut a long story short, I was working and Seth was supposed to be working. Instead, he was going over to my babysitter's house. He would walk her boyfriend to where he was going, then double back to the house, use our son to get in and try to sleep with the babysitter.

Sometimes, he would go over after work and hang out with the boyfriend. He would wait for him to leave the room, and would then try and hit on Vanessa. She was terrified of him, but she also didn't want me to be upset with her. We had a mutual friend who lived downstairs, who assured Vanessa that she could talk to me. Low and behold, when she called me, he had left work at lunchtime and she hid the phone so that he wouldn't see it—I heard everything.

The Nook

My first reaction was the hurt, but then my heart sank into the pit of my stomach because it took me back to the times that I was violated. This girl was only about seventeen years old, so the first thing that came to my mind was how developed my daughter Chaundivia was and had he touched my baby? I was frantic the whole day after the phone call. I desperately wanted to get home and question my child. When I got home I asked her, and she said no. I was relieved, but he still had to go. That night, when he came home, I asked him about it and told him what I had heard. I told him that I didn't want to be with him anymore and I asked him if he was even sorry. He told me the only thing that he was sorry for, was that he had been caught. I'm laughing now, but my goodness I wanted to slit that man's throat.

The next morning, I got up and pretended to leave for work. When he left, I went back into the house and started packing up every item in the house that belonged to him. I didn't care about what I had to let go of, as far as I was concerned, we would do without it—I just wanted him gone.

When I had removed most of his stuff out of the house, I went to Kmart and purchased new locks. I returned home, changed the locks and put the rest of his furniture, clothes and TVs on the porch. I waited for him to get home and called his parole officer and told him, "Your parolee is no longer welcome in my home, and please advise him to get away from my house or the police will be called." I passed the phone out the window so that he could talk to his officer and make the necessary arrangements.

Aden happened after Seth. Now after my mother passed, Church was a hit or miss kind of thing but hooking up with Aden led me to Tiny, and Tiny led me back to God. Things were good for a few months. This all happened after one day, while lying in bed, my daughter asked me when we were going back to church. A few weeks later, there was a death in Aden's family and he wanted to go to church so we started attending the church where his cousin's funeral was held. There was something different about this church. The worship touched my soul, and it was that very worship that was changing me. One day Aden suggested that we stop fornicating until we got married—and I agreed.

Three months later he was cheating and I politely packed his things. I didn't need to talk, I didn't want to hear a word, I was fed up and I had had ENOUGH!

What happened to Aden? God happened to Aden!

Chapter 7

GOD'S PLAN

*For I know the plans I have for you," declares the LORD, "plans to prosper you and not to harm you,
plans to give you hope and a future.*
JEREMIAH 29:11 (*NIV*)

Aden no longer went to Elim Christian Fellowship, so of course we stopped going to Elim, and started going back to our old church, Free Spirit.

By this time, Tiny had a little girl by Bill. Somehow, we connected for her to braid my hair and I was drawn to her spirit. While braiding my hair, we started talking and I shared with her all that was going on. I was actually still with Aden at the time and was engaged to be married. Before I left, she invited me to come back to her house for a prayer. Every now and then, we would get together to pray or talk on the phone.

Overtime, events drew us closer together. Aden and I had broken up and Bill was murdered. Bill and I weren't together, but I was sad all the same because Bill was a great dad to Dejahnique, and still helped with my other two girls. Once he and I broke up, we started getting along well. If I needed help with paying a bill, clothes for the kids or even food, he took care of it. Whatever the need was, it didn't matter. I could call him for anything and he was right there, no questions asked, regardless of our situation.

I started going back to Elim with Tiny for Tuesday night Bible studies, but I was still attending Free Spirit on Sundays. The worship at Elim had me hooked, so I started going to the 7am Sunday service and going to Free Spirit afterwards.

    One night, while I was asleep, there was a thunderstorm and I woke up. I could hear God saying, "This is where I want you." Now this was something new for me, so I questioned it and didn't move. I prayed and asked God for some confirmation. A few nights later, I was asleep on the couch and I had a dream about the Pastor of Elim. We were at the amusement park, standing in a line. Then he turned to me, and asked me if I would accompany him on this journey. In the midst of this, God made it uncomfortable at Free Spirit, nothing was moving me anymore; neither the worship nor the Word. Finally, I told my pastor that I had to go and that I believed that God was moving me somewhere else. This man was not happy and he did not release me with his blessings—but I was following God.

    Even though I had left Free Spirit, the dreams increased. He sent dreams to warn me that trials were coming and dreams to show me my growth. I was dreaming on a regular basis and it was exciting. One night, Tiny invited me to go with her to a prayer meeting at Pastor Marcia's house. While she was teaching, the Spirit hit her and she started prophesying. When she got to me, I started getting hot. My hands and my face felt like they were being scorched with fire. They were so hot, and I couldn't shake that heat off.

    Now do you remember the vision of the little girl in the street? She started to tell me, "There is healing in your hands, to heal the sick and raise the dead." Just then I saw the vision of the little girl and was slain in the spirit.

    As I lay there, I had no clue about what was happening to me but they started to remove my shoes, and as Pastor Marcia anointed my feet, she kept prophesying over me about going to the nations and jurisdictional authority. When I got up she said, "God has called you His prophetess, I want you to read the book of Acts every day for the rest of the week and ask God for your tongues." WHAT? HUH?

I got home and had to have a serious talk with Jesus. Like, "Okay, Lord, now hold on one Holy rolling moment. This lady has confirmed that I'm not cuckoo for cocoa puffs. And I truly appreciate it, Lord, but please, I need you to explain all of that mumbo-jumbo that this lady was talking about. What is a prophetess? And why on earth did I pass out like that? And why was she oiling my feet using all these words I had never heard in my life?" Grandma Alberta prayed to beads; and the family church as well as Free Spirit were Baptist so I'd never heard stuff like this. God answered through Acts, dreams and the Bible study that following week, plus Tiny helped me out by explaining some of what Pastor Marcia was saying. I was really excited now and ready to be used by God. I read the book of Acts twice a day for a whole two weeks.

One day, during Sunday service, I heard God tell me to go to the Altar. You know that I was a baby because I tried to reason with God. I told Him, *"Father, I don't know the protocol. I don't think I'm supposed to be moving right now."* Just then I got a flash of Pastor Marcia's face and my heart started to race and my body started shaking hard. I was so scared, I thought God was about to kill me like one of the Israelites! I pushed past all the kids and shoved Tiny out the way, and as soon as I stepped out into the aisle, Pastor Marcia stood up from her seat and was standing at the end of the aisle, waiting for me.

I walked up to the altar so fast and fell on it. She knelt down beside me and told me not to think about it, but to start saying what I was hearing. I was speaking in tongues and crying. I had sweat pouring off of me like someone had poured a bucket of water on me. When I got back to my seat, I tried to sit down but the Spirit was on me so powerful that I couldn't be still. My kids were looking at me in fear and before I knew it, I started laying my hands on them and the whole row caught on fire. I had been baptized in the Holy Spirit, and it was the greatest feeling in the world.

When I got home I was so tired that I lay down. I must have slept for about twenty minutes and I was back up and at it again. I was speaking in tongues all day and well into the night, I went to bed speaking in tongues. At about two o'clock in the morning, I heard someone call my name. When I opened my eyes, the devil threw a huge spider at me. I jumped up, screamed so loudly and started speaking in tongues again.

Now back then I was terrified of spiders, so this thing bothered me until I talked to Pastor Marcia the next day. She told me the enemy was angry and not to worry about it but just keep praying in tongues every day. This happened in August 2004.

A few weeks later, I had a dream about a tornado hitting my house. In the background, there were fighter jets landing, one and then two, one and then two at a time—they just kept landing. As the tornado hit my house, my house shook but nothing was damaged. I got up and went outside and everything was torn up except the perimeter around my house. God told me that a storm was coming, that the fighter jets that I had seen in my dreams were my angels, and that my children and I would be okay as long as I stayed close to Him.

A week later, I had two garnishments (debt collection): one for a student loan and one the IRS. I only had enough to pay my tithe, rent and lights. A week later, my gas was cut off; and a few days later we had a bad storm. I pressed into God like never before. At that time, when I read the Bible, I would have an open vision like I was there right in the middle of the Bible. This made me read and study even more. It was a testing of my faith and I was growing stronger every minute. Though some days, I was strong and some days, I was a mess, crying and asking God why this was happening. My bedroom and the kids' bedrooms were in the back of the apartment. The house was freezing cold, so I closed off the doorway to the front of the house with plastic and a blanket. I had a heater in the back to keep the bedrooms warm, and I made the kids stay in the back.

    I used hot plates to cook meals and boil water for baths. This was rough and I have to admit, some days I wanted to quit because I couldn't understand why in the world I had to go through this just to serve God. I thought that just saying yes was enough—He would use me and I would be happy. And when I got to a breaking point, I would have a vision or a dream of what was to come and I would have hope again.

    One time I had separated my bill money, as I always did. I paid the landlord, then went and paid the light bill. But when I got ready to pay my tithe, there was $425 left—the amount of my rent. I paid my tithe and when I got home I called the landlord and asked him if I had given him the wrong amount by mistake. He said no, I had given him $425. I hung up that phone and started screaming, "Hallelujah! Hallelujah! Thank you, God!" He had blessed me with extra money that I didn't even ask for. There was also another time when the kids and I were starting to run low on food. I was in a prayer group one Thursday night and had been paid. My plan was to go get groceries the next day, but God had a better plan. That night, one of the ladies in the group testified that she had lost her job a few weeks back, and had no idea where her next meal was coming from, but she was trusting in God. I said to God in my head, *"Lord I have to help her. I know we are only running low on food but we are not out yet."* I felt terrible, so I asked God to bless my giving and I placed a $100 seed into her hands.

The Nook

That night I went home, got the kids fed and into bed. Just as I finished my prayers and climbed into bed, I got a text message: "For the next 6 months, I am going to give you $150 in stamps." I was so excited! I jumped up out of that bed and started dancing, crying and thanking God.

At that time, I was working 11 am to 7 pm. However, the next day, when I got to work, I was told that an 8:30-4:30 shift had opened up and I could have it. Also, that overtime was opened and I was eligible to work it. By the first week in December, I had made enough money to pay off the gas bill and have the gas turned back on. I learned to trust and depend on God and my faith was growing stronger.

My life had taken a complete 180 degree turn and things were getting better for the kids and me. I was getting to know and falling in love with Jesus. I had stopped smoking marijuana, I stopped drinking hard liquor but would still have the occasional glass of wine. As far as going out clubbing, I only went out when it was a sibling or family member's birthday. I was even working on my potty-mouth. This was extremely difficult and took much prayer and discipline because everyone I knew had a filthy mouth— including my mother and grandmother.

Believe it or not, I had even given up fornication. I was no longer attracted to bad boys but I wanted a godly man. I knew that I had to clean myself up in order to get one. I was beginning to like myself, heck, I was even beginning to love myself and the person that I was becoming. I had even started trusting that good things could happen to me, as long as I stayed focused and continued to serve God.

Sure, I had some troubles along the way, but so did my favorite Bible character David. So every time bad things would happen in my life, I would park my studies in 1st & 2nd Samuel and 1st &

GOD'S PLAN

2nd Kings; as well as the book of Psalms to bring myself peace. Everyone has their thing that gets them over the hurdles during hard times and for me this was it—it still is to this very day.

I was single and celibate for about two years before I met Mr. Christian at a gas station. I was struggling to put air in my tires and Eli got out of his car and asked me, in Spanish, if he could help. I told him that I didn't speak Spanish and he asked me again in English. I used to get offended when people assumed that I was Puerto Rican, but by the time I had reached my early to mid-twenties it no longer bothered me. Plus, it was so darn cold, I quickly said yes, passed him the hose and hopped into my heated vehicle. Don't judge me! Buffalo can get bitter cold in the winter, and after that year where I had to go without heat for two months, I couldn't stand to be cold, not even for a moment. After Eli took care of my tires he asked me where my husband was. I should have sped off, but I told him that I was single and "I am black, just so you know". When he asked if he could call me, my first question was, "Do you believe in Jesus?" He said yes. "Do you attend a church?" He said yes and then told me the name of his church as well as his pastor's name. He asked me to get out so that he could show me something, and when I got out of the van, he took my hand and led me back to his car. He opened the door and reached in and pulled out his Bible with a church bulletin.

I had seen his Pastor before. I knew him as one of my Pastor's spiritual sons who had preached at Elim several times. There was only one question left, "Are you single?" "Yes, what kind of man do you take me for". I was like putty in his hands. I remember thinking that I had never dated a Puerto Rican man before so maybe he would be different from the men I had dated in the past. Plus, I had been single for two years and here was this good-looking, godly man who wanted to date me. Problem is, I didn't have a clue as to how to date successfully without compromising my celibacy.

The Nook

We were dating for a few months and things were going great. Sometimes he would come over to my place and we would study together. I was amazed at how much he knew and I was attracted to his wisdom. He taught me things about the Bible that I didn't know, and if we didn't see each other he would always make sure to call me so we could pray together before we went to bed. I was falling for this man in the worst way and before I knew it, that lustful spirit started rising up.

It was Valentine's Day. Eli had never dated a black girl before, so he asked if we could do dinner at the house. He would make some Spanish food and I was going to make some soul food. After dinner, we sat in the front room and he played his guitar for me for the first time and because the kids were gone, he stayed late. Mistake number one: we were in the house alone. Mistake number two: we were drinking wine.

Before we knew it, one kiss had led to us fornicating. I cried like a baby and he kept telling me he was sorry, but I didn't want to hear that—I wanted my cleanliness back! I'm not all that sure of what could have become of our relationship but I felt that Eli was a threat to all that I loved, so I broke it off with him. I changed my number and ignored the door when he came over to talk. I didn't know how to fix what we had done and I was not about to risk losing what I had with God—so I denied myself and walked away. It was another three years before I met and allowed another man to get close to me.

Chapter 8

ADDICTED

*The godly may trip seven times,
but they will get up again.
But one disaster is enough
to overthrow the wicked.
Proverbs 24:16 (NLT)*

Some people are blessed enough to have parents that take them to church every time the church doors are open. Whether they went willingly, or kicking and screaming, they still got churched. I only had Grandma Hazel to take me to church. I appreciate her taking me because I went just enough for her to plant the seed of salvation in my heart. However, it wasn't nearly enough for me to learn Kingdom principles.

I am by no means knocking anyone but as I started going to church on my own, I often thought back to one particular day, when we were children, and my aunt had something like a mock wedding. (A Tom Thumb Wedding) Instead of kissing the boy, she slapped him, and he chased her around the church. And to this day I have wondered, what the heck was that all about? I have often wondered what my life would have been like if I had parents to take me to church every Sunday. Heck! I have often wondered how different my life could have been had I had parents. Period. And I have regretted it all of my life.

There was so much that I didn't understand when it came to the Bible and what being saved really and truly entailed. So, when the opportunity arose for me to attend the Sound of the Genuine Biblical Institute, I wanted in. Our pastor introduced it as an inductive Bible Study, I didn't know exactly what that was but I was interested and I needed all the Bible Study that I could get. However, the classes cost money and I needed permission from God, so instantly I took it to God in prayer. The first answer of "yes" came that same week by way of a dream. I dreamt that I was graduating and walking across the stage. This was something that I had never done before. Remember I finished high school by way of summer school and my diploma was mailed to me. The following week I had a dream that the Pastor was in front of me and he turned around and asked me, "You haven't gotten your butt off that couch for class yet?" That Tuesday, during Bible study, I went and paid for my class.

Two weeks later, I was in class. I was determined and focused. A man was the last thing on my mind—and that's when my van broke down. I freaking hate the devil! By this time my 2nd oldest daughter had just had a baby. I was taking the bus to work, church and my classes, and some days I had to drag my youngest daughter, son and grandchild with me on the bus. One day, it was pouring after church and I was at the bus stop with the kids. One of the guys from the church was driving past, and he stopped and asked if I needed a ride. He seemed harmless enough, and he and Tiny always laughed and talked after church, so I said yes.

We realized that he lived two blocks away from me, so he offered to take us back and forth to church every week, so I agreed. I was very standoffish at first. I was polite and I gave him conversation, but I kept it short! Wilbur hit it off with my son and my granddaughter loved him, so it wasn't long before he started stopping by the house to see the kids. We would sit on the porch, sometimes for hours. I relaxed and let down my guard and we got comfortable with just being friends at first.

I was in Year 2 of the Sound of the Genuine Biblical Institute, and things were going well. Until—I hooked up with ungodly council. I started hanging out with a girl named Shelly. She and I went to the same church, but we knew each other from a past affiliation. Honestly, I think our demons of lust attracted us to one another. We were complete opposites and she was still drinking, partying and fornicating. She explained it as "God knows our hearts. He knows we are going to sin, so He forgives us." When she asked me about Wilbur, I told her that he had expressed interest in me, but I was older than him and I didn't think it was a good idea. She told me, "Girl that boy is grown. You need to stop being scared and go for it." Every time she and I got together, she asked me if we had hooked up yet.

A little leaven leaveneth the whole lump. Galatians 5:9 (*KJV*). This girl was bad news and I wish I had the discernment to know that before I started getting in too deep with her. Before I knew it, I was hanging out with her at the bar having drinks. I had also moved and allowed Wilbur to move from the "just friends" category.

Here we go again—I was back in sin, fornicating and drinking. Wilbur lived with his dad, but after his dad passed away, within a few months, we were shacking up. I felt no guilt—I treated it like it was normal, and because so many of my new friends in the church were doing it, it had to be okay, right? After all God knows my heart. The soul tie between this man and myself was so strong, that even when he got busted cheating, I didn't leave him. I was in a serious rut.

You see, I was saved and had given my life to Christ—but I didn't know that I had to be delivered from the roots of molestation. I didn't know that what had opened the door to lust was still in me, lying dormant, waiting for its opportunity to strike and cause me to stumble. It had reared its ugly head and I had been sucked back in again.

The Nook

From the start, one of the biggest problems with this relationship was that even though I wanted Wilbur, I was falling in love with God, so I struggled off and on with the issue of fornication. I had such guilt all the time and when I wanted to stop, it was difficult, because the urge to commit the act was always there. Even when I slept, I dreamt about it and some nights I woke up and gave in to it. I felt horrible and prayed often, "Lord I'm so sorry. Please forgive me. And if you forgive me I'll never do it again." And I even prayed for God to completely take my sexual desire away—but it never happened.

We argued all the time and it was driving me nuts. It seemed that everything I did made him angry. Some days we had been in church and just come out of a seriously high praise session, I'm talking "the Pastor couldn't even get up to preach," type of praise and after that, all I wanted to do was come home and take one of those "after church" naps, but Wilbur wanted to argue.

Some days I wanted to take a knife and plunge it into his heart because he didn't know how to just say what was on his mind and let it go. He would drag it on with one example explained in fifty different ways. We would get home from church at 10 am and some days it would be 2am in the morning and this man would still be going on about the same thing. I had to be at work in the morning, so some days I would just sit quietly stewing inside and on other days my patience wore thin and I would explode. One day, we got into an argument and he blurted out, "Nobody wants your fat butt but me. Why do you think you've got all these kids and never been married?" I couldn't take it. I exploded, "Mother bleeper I don't need you! You can be replaced at any moment! Men try to talk to me all the time, I just never tell you!"

That thing must have really struck a nerve. I'm not sure if God was showing me how much I had changed or not, but this dude knocked the heck out of me and when I went to reach for the phone, he jumped on my back and bit me in my face. I fought him off long enough to call the police and when they arrived, I had him arrested.

By the time he got out of jail, I had a restraining order against him—which was completely pointless because that lasted about a good three weeks before he was back at the house with me again. I can't, for the life of me, tell you why I stayed with this man. He was mentally, physically and verbally abusive, and out of all the relationships I have ever had, he was the only one I tolerated disrespect from. I never allowed a man to call me out my name, and Fat B was his favorite name for me every time he got ticked off.

I sank deeper into my studies and God was still blessing me, in spite of all of my sins. I got a promotion, a new/used vehicle and I was still growing in the church in leaps and bounds, and so were my children. Wilbur and I were making plans to get married, so we moved from my apartment into project housing to save money. I graduated from Sound of the Genuine and I was finally strong enough to express my concerns about Wilbur and me no longer having sex until we got married. He agreed, but he was having sex with another lady—behind my back. We were in the new place for maybe six months before I received a call from that lady saying that she was pregnant—I was livid. I called my brother to come over and put Wilbur out. I think this time he was gone for two months before I let him back in. I started to notice that I was very angry, and was easily set off by anything, and if he came at me I was ready to throw down. I didn't pay attention to how much this was troubling my children.

This pattern went on with us for the whole five years that we were together, and so did the fornication pattern. We would stop, break up, then get back together and it would start again. Things became so bad that my youngest daughter started acting out and I reached out to the youth pastor.

The Nook

I started going to counseling sessions. During one of these sessions, I realized that there was something wrong with me when one of the pastors asked me two questions. He asked me, "What is it that you are so afraid of—is it being alone? And what is it that is causing you to devalue yourself?"

These two questions provoked me deep into thought. It wasn't until these questions were asked, that I started to ask God, *"What am I so afraid of? And what is it that is causing me to devalue myself?"* It was then that I learned that molestations can cause many different things to happen to a person. But for me, it was promiscuity and an addiction to sexual perversion. I had to get rid of this... and quickly, so I started fasting and praying often. The last two times that Wilbur and I had fooled around, I believe that the Holy Spirit was starting to deal with me, because I felt such guilt and I cried the whole time. Finally, I just couldn't take it anymore and told him "that's it" until we got married.

In the midst of us planning to get married, I had taken part in an anger management Bible Study at another church. Their bible study was on Thursdays, so it made it easy to go. After the classes were over, I purchased the CD's and listened to them every day while at work. Little-by-little, I was being set free from anger. And I was also drifting apart from Wilbur.

One day we got into a really bad argument and I told God if He got me out of the relationship this time, I would never go back. Wilbur enlisted in the military and they stationed him in many states away from me. However, because I was still struggling with the soul tie, we stayed together. When he came home on leave, we set up marriage counseling, and moved forward in our plans to get married. Until one day, I saw an email from another woman. I emailed her back, and it made Wilbur angry. We argued all night. The whole time he was home on leave, he was up in my face screaming and spitting, and when I asked him to stop, he did it more. I remember thinking the military made this guy "brave". I held my tongue but after two weeks of that mess, I couldn't take it anymore—in my mind it was over. I couldn't wait for him to leave and the minute I dropped him off and returned home, I went throughout the whole house and gathered every picture that I had of him. I put them on the grill and I burned them, and asked God to sever the relationship. Huh... God knows my heart. Yes! God knows your heart that's why He desires to give you a new heart!

So I stopped calling him and cut all ties. I deleted everyone on Facebook that were mutual friends, I blocked him, changed my number and went on a 21-day water fast to break the soul tie.

There was a singles minister on Facebook and I started following him and learning how to be successfully single. It's been over five years and I have not looked back. I thank God for setting me free from that bondage. And even more than that, I thank God for deliverance. When people ask me how do I stay celibate? Or how do I fight the urge to fornicate? I tell them I pray, "Lord keep me in all of my ways." I fast to crucify my flesh and I, once in a while, also allow myself to remember all the things that God has brought me out of. The memories alone shut every lustful thought down! I must say that God has been faithful to keep me, and for that I am eternally grateful.

Now to Him who is able to keep you from stumbling,
and to make you stand in the presence of His glory blameless
with great joy,
to the only God our Savior,
through Jesus Christ our Lord,
be glory, majesty, dominion and authority,
before all time and now and forever.
Amen.
Jude 24-25 (*NASB*)

Chapter 9

MORE THAN A CONQUEROR

...in all these things we are more than conquerors
through him who loved us.
Romans 8:37 (*NIV*)

After this relationship ended, I had to be healed. I was so broken inside that I was truly no good to anyone. The devil had me right where he wanted me. I was called to people yet I didn't want anything to do with anyone. I just wanted to be left alone. There are some things that happen in your life that can cause you to fall into a deep rut where all you can do is self-medicate. After this relationship was over, I medicated myself with comfort foods and blew up like a hot air balloon. And finally, I came to realize that I was miserable—I needed help and I needed deliverance.

One of the first things God did was He made me feel so uncomfortable at Elim, that when He told me to move I didn't put up a fight. I moved over to a little storefront church that was run by a husband and wife who operated in the prophetic and deliverance ministry. It was now time to get healed, get delivered and get refocused. This was not an easy process at all. One of the hardest things to do is change your mindset from victim to vindicated when you've been a victim for so long.

I feel that the key to this type of deliverance rests solely on your acceptance of all that has taken place, and your willingness to work hard at forgiveness. Not just forgiveness for those who have wounded you, but to forgive yourself.

The Nook

For me I had to do some serious soul searching. I needed to first admit that I had a problem with me so that I could release myself and give myself permission to be free. One of the biggest problems was that I had buried most of those painful events in my life so deep within my heart, that prayer and fasting were needed. I had to rely on the Holy Spirit to reveal to me what was hidden in my heart. I thought that I had forgiven everyone, but the truth of the matter was that I had not—all I had really accomplished was suppressing my emotions by burying them and covering them up with sex, alcohol, marijuana and food. The first thing that needed work—was me.

I needed to forgive myself and learn to love myself. I couldn't stand my shape, my skin complexion and some of my other body parts. I took a vow of celibacy before God and I committed myself to making daily affirmations. When I went into the bathroom the first thing I saw was short prayer that I had printed out and taped to the mirror "LORD PLEASE ALLOW ME TO SEE MYSELF AS YOU SEE ME" and every time I went into the bathroom, I repeated this prayer. I remember one day, a while since my mother had passed away, I was in the bathroom washing my face and when I looked into the mirror I said, "Wow! I really am cute." I must have laughed for a good fifteen minutes.

It wasn't until I read The Purpose Driven Life by Rick Warren, as well as Captivated by John & Stasi Eldridge that I began to LOVE myself and appreciate every inch of who God formed and fashioned me to be. My nose wasn't so big any more, it was perfect; it was the nose that my God had chosen for me to have. And my feet were no longer flat, fat and ugly but they were the feet that God saw fit to bless me with. And my body- my shape was not a pervert magnet. It was fearfully and wonderfully made and designed by God.

I didn't know until I was reading Sophia Ruffin's book from Point Guard to Prophet that I was still harboring anger towards my mother for not being there in my life when I needed her; as well as for not believing me when I told her that John had tried to rape me. But I had to acknowledge and confess what I felt, and not just towards her, but towards my dad as well.

One day, I was on the floor during a service, spitting up and crying so hard that I burst some blood vessels in my cheeks. I heard God say to me, "When you call your dad and forgive him, it will be finished." I was hot, why couldn't I just call out his name and forgive him by God's Spirit? There was no answer! I got home and I cried some more because I did not want to call this man. I had rolled around on the floor, spat up and everything. Why couldn't I be delivered and that be it? It took me a few hours to get up the nerve to call my dad. Finally, when I realized that no one was going pick up the phone and pep talk me to do it, I called. I was praying that he wouldn't answer so that I could hang up and say, "See God? He didn't pick up." And on the forth ring he picked up.
"Hello?"
"Hi Dad, how are you?"
"Hey, Baby, I'm fine. How are you?"
"I'm doing good, how have you been?"
"Pretty good, just came in from picking some tomatoes in the garden. What's up?"
"Dad, I called because I have some things that I have to say to you."
"What is it Baby?"
I took a deep breath, "I called because I need to forgive you."
"Forgive me for what?"
"Dad this is hard for me, please, just let me get this out."
"Okay, go ahead Baby."
"I need to tell you that I forgive you because I felt like you never loved me like you loved the others. And, also, I felt like you didn't protect me from Uncle Tom. I felt like it was some of your fault, what happened to me."

The Nook

"I understand about your uncle and I'm sorry about what happened to you. That hurt me bad, but Baby I never knew you felt like that about me not loving you. I am so sorry. I never knew!" By now I am fighting back the tears.

"I forgive you Dad, but now I also need to ask for your forgiveness because I intentionally tried to hurt you by asking Uncle George to give me away when I was getting married."

"It's okay Baby, I forgive you."

"Thank you Daddy.", the tears were flowing now, "Okay, it's late and I have to get to bed for work in the morning."

"Okay Baby, talk to you later—I love you."

"I love you too Daddy."

    I got off that phone and cried like a baby! It took me over an hour to contain myself. When I got up that next morning and went into the bathroom, I looked into the mirror, turned and made a beeline back to my bedroom and picked up the phone. I called in and booked myself off from work because there was no way I was going to work looking like that!

    My eyes were almost swollen shut from all that crying and my cheeks had a bunch of red dots from the broken blood vessels. I looked as if Mike Tyson had just whooped my behind. I ran my gel mask under the cold water, put it on my eyes and went back to bed! Later that day, I got a call from Dad to see how I was doing. We talked for a good minute and when we hung up, I started crying again and thanking God. Even though the calling each other only lasted a few days, I was grateful that I was able to express my feelings and get healing from the hurt and pain that had kept me bound for so many years.

    My uncle had passed away long before this healing process had taken place, so my healing came a different way. I bumped in to my cousin whom I had not seen in a while, and she asked me if I had attended Uncle Tom's funeral. I told her no, and that I couldn't bring myself to go. That's when she confessed that Uncle Tom had molested her and some other girls in the family. I paid a visit to my aunt to ask her about it and sure enough, I was not the only one. But I was one of many victims including his sisters. One aunt admitted to sleeping with a knife and pulling it out on him so he never got a chance to hurt her. Several of his nieces and a few cousins had been victimized by his perversion. The waterworks started when I told her about me. By the time I got home, I felt such a freedom and a peace. I called out his name, "Uncle Tom, I forgive you." Then I said my prayers, laid down and went to sleep.

    A year had passed and I was really growing, I had preached at two churches and was being used by God. However, some things were starting to take place at the church that were starting to make me seriously uncomfortable, so my prayer partner and I started praying, and I fasted several times for God to release me to a new church home.

    Three months later, He released me. When I got up that morning for church, I heard the Holy Spirit tell me to go to Edison Street Community Church, but I thought it was my flesh trying to lead me back to something familiar; a place of comfort, because I was familiar with and had known Pastor Ted as one of Bishop Bronner's spiritual sons from my previous church Elim. So I got up, got dressed and went to my cousin's church as usual, but there was no one there, and I heard God say, "I told you to go to Edison." So, I got back into my van and off I went to where I was told to go.

    From the moment I walked into the doors, I felt as if I was home. It seemed like I was at the altar every other week and I was tired of it. I was like, *"Dear God! How much junk do I have in there because every time I turn around, I'm rolling around on the floor!"* What I didn't know and understand was that some of the events in my life were caused by generational curses that were allowed to travel from one generation to the next. God showed me that my dad couldn't be like other dads because his dad was never present in his life to teach him how to be a dad. My dad didn't know how to properly protect me because he was bound by a curse passed down from one generation to the next. Growing up in those days you did what you were told, so when the embarrassment of rape and molestation hit a family, the rule was "what happens in this house stays in this house."

John 8:32 says *"And ye shall know the truth, and the truth shall make thee free."* When a family does not open up and talk about the demons that are running rampant and plaguing their lives, they give that demon permission and power to keep visiting the next generation.

On my father's side, it was lust, perversion and poverty, as well as a few other demons that hinder growth and acceleration in the things of God. It took me a while before I could even share what happened to me with anyone— my children were the first. When I started dealing with generational curses, God had me call a family dinner where I got all of my children together and we talked about all that had happened to me. In the midst of that meeting, it came out that one daughter had been raped as well as molested, and one was almost raped. My heart was broken and I repented to each of my children for allowing the curse to touch their lives. This opened up the door for healing, but it also taught me how to pray and stop the cycle from repeating itself and touching my grandchildren, going down ten generations.

I feel that people are so afraid of how rape or molestation reflects on them as a parent and caregiver, that they silence the victim from exposing the violation; not knowing that by silencing the victim, they are creating a level of shame in the victim that could have been avoided if there was an open and safe line of communication. It's not until we begin to talk about the hurt that healing is able to take place.

There was so much that I had to overcome through the years and I am still conquering demons to this day. Even though the things from my past have hurt me deeply, I wouldn't change a thing because I understand that everything that God allowed me to survive was for my children, grandchildren and maybe even you, the one reading this book right now.

I'M A SURVIVOR AND SO ARE YOU!

Chapter 10

BEAUTY FOR ASHES

> To appoint unto them that mourn in Zion,
> to give unto them beauty for ashes,
> the oil of joy for mourning,
> the garment of praise for the spirit of heaviness;
> that they might be called trees of righteousness, the planting of
> the Lord, that he might be glorified.
> Isaiah 61:3 (*KJV*)

When my mother was home, every other Saturday was hair day. She would take my hair down and then wash and braid it in what seemed like 1000 tiny and painful braids. It felt like, with each tug of the hair, she was ripping me bald. If that wasn't enough torture, she couldn't grease my scalp until the braids were done because the grease would prevent her from getting a good grip on the hair, so I had to sit through the painful process of her greasing my scalp to protect my hair from drying out and breaking off. After all of that was done, I couldn't lay on my head for the first two nights. I would have to prop my hands under my cheeks and sleep like that. And if I had anything to say about the pain, she would always tell me, "Baby, beauty hurts." Mama wasn't lying.

Some of the deliverance that I have walked through has truly been painful. I remember when I was in Nigeria, and the apostle had an altar call; I was not going up to that altar! *"Lord I did not come all these miles to cut a fool in front of these people."* Well, by the time he had finished, there were three things that I needed to receive prayer for, so I made my way to the altar.

The Nook

As soon as I got up there and the apostle started praying, I began crying. I gasped for air and I had an excruciating sharp pain in my chest and then I felt something snap in my chest, I fell to my knees and whispered, "Lord, please don't kill me in Nigeria." I thought I was having a heart attack. Then I heard the word *deliverance*. I took another deep breath, lifted my hands and said, "Thank You Jesus!".

I think it was two days later that they did another altar call to break generational curses. I kid you not! I started sweating, and just then a woman in red appeared in front of me. She screamed and fell backwards and I fell down under the power. When the man of God was done praying, I tried to get up because I didn't want to be the only one on the floor when everyone was gone. I reached up to one of the girls from my church to grab my hand, but I was so limp that they had to drag me back to my seat. When they sat me in the chair, I was leaning over the chair as if I had been drinking. That was the second time that I had experienced being drunk in the Spirit. About an hour later they called everyone from America back up to the altar for prayer. I think I lasted ten minutes before I fell down again.

When I got back to my seat, I said, "Come on God, my pastor is never going to take me anywhere else. I have been on that floor since I been here. Did you really bring me this far to keep knocking me out?"

We got back to our house and they ribbed on me so bad, that all I could do was laugh. Now, even though I was embarrassed about spending so much time on the floor, I was grateful because God was uprooting some things in me, breaking some things off of me, as well as healing me.

One day, after we returned back to America, while in Bible study, I was laughing and talking with someone, and my pastor walked by and said, "Chaundria your smile is different." I remember thinking, *"Wow God! That must have been some serious deliverance to change my smile."*

I'm still walking out my deliverance from some things. I never would have imagined that there was so much that a person would need to be delivered from. One day, I was talking to my pastor who told me something to the extent that the longer we live, the more we take on of the world. When I pondered on that I received this revelation:

From the time we are children, sin enters in. It's almost like starting out skinny, but over the years the things that we eat tend to add extra cushion on our body and if we never slow up and change our eating habits, some of us become obese. However, when we do decide to lose that weight, the one thing that we must first do is change our mindsets, then we have to change our diets and gradually start to exercise—building momentum.

The same thing is true for deliverance and walking in holiness. We must learn to make deliverance a part of a healthy lifestyle—eliminating things that are bad for us, things like certain TV shows, certain music and even some of the places that we visit—and replacing those bad things with things that are good for us. I am nowhere close to perfect and there are still some shows that I do like to watch. However, at least once to twice a week, I utilize prayers from Apostle John Eckhardt's book *Prayers that Rout Demons2*.

I thank God for deliverance. When I look back over all that I have been through and see where I am now, sometimes I tear up, while other times I can't do anything but thank God and worship Him. If it had not been for God, I don't know where I would be today—I could have easily been dead.

The Nook

    But He chose to pick me up, wash me off and give me beauty for ashes. I'm not where I want to be yet, but I'm so glad that I am not what, and where, I used to be—and I look forward to where God is taking me. In the midst of my transition, I have learned that it's okay to give myself permission to be happy and it's also okay for me to give myself permission to live life on purpose and to the fullest.

Depression free,
guilt free.
bondage free—
unapologetically!

Chapter 11

FROM DARKNESS TO LIGHT

*You are my hiding place;
you will protect me from trouble and surround me with songs of deliverance.
Psalm 32: 7 (NIV)*

I remember that there was a time when I couldn't stand to be in a room without the television playing or loud music blaring, because I couldn't stand to be alone with my thoughts, and I was my least favorite person to be around. However, when I started to receive deliverance and moved from liking myself to loving myself, it was nothing to drive home without music or sit in a dark room and relax in silence.

The Nook for me started out in my grandmother's closet, but because the trauma was too great for me to deal with, the Nook became the deep recesses of my heart, buried and covered up by emotional behaviors.

Today the Nook is a big brown double-sized chair that I cuddle up in. Some days, when I am lonely or hurting, I climb into my chair and I invite Daddy God in, asking Him to hold me as I dim the lights, put on some worship music and fall asleep in the safety of the Master's arms.

Some days this Nook is a place of refuge, some days a place of comfort, while other days it's a place of refreshing. No matter what it is that I am in need of, I know that if I can just get home to our meeting place, that the Father is faithful to meet me there, and fill my cup to the point of overflow.

The Nook

It's in this place that I can be me and reveal my heart to the Father to see the hurt and pain, the victories gained and every vulnerable feeling that needs His attention. Some days I can call Him and He comes right away, and other days I have to tarry and wait—but there hasn't been a time that I haven't invited Him in, that my Father didn't show up to my big brown chair—better known as my Nook.

CONCLUSION

There was a man who looked past my sin,
and saw the potential in me.
He loved me so much that He left his throne and volunteered to suffer
the most gruesome death to save me.
He bore the weight of my sins
and
He hung, bled and died on a cross.
From that moment on,
my eyes were opened to see
because He went straight to hell
and took back the keys,
that made me free.
He ascended back into Heaven
and he's seated at the right hand of the Father
He is the LION of the tribe of Judah.
He is My King.
HEAR HIM ROAR!

Once upon a time,
there was a girl
who found her worth in
JESUS.

THE END.

MY CLOSING PRAYER

Most Loving God,

Writing this has caused me to process every pain from my childhood, just as I am sure it reopened the wounds of the readers. While it may be hard for them to understand the why's of their circumstances, I pray, even now, that You will allow them to see that which was meant for evil, You desire to use for Your glory.

I thank You, even now Father, that You are removing the spirit of shame from each and every person.

Most Loving God, she or he was severely wounded—hurt beyond words. The betrayal of trust, coupled with the physical abuse, has left them shattered—unable to trust and experience love the way You have desired.

Father, I pray now that as You begin the healing process, that You will release courage to forgive, and restore trust and confidence to love again.

But more than anything, I pray Father God, that You will give them a Holy Ghost boldness to tell their story, so that another may be healed, delivered and set free as they break free from the chains of bondage.

In Jesus' Name,
   Amen

REFERENCES

1. **Eckhardt, Apostle John**. Destroying the Spirit of Rejection: Receive Love and Acceptance and Find Healing. 2017.

2. **Eckhardt, John**. Prayers that Rout Demons. 2007.

Scriptures to Cling to for Healing and Deliverance:

John 8:36 (King James Version)
If the Son therefore shall make you free, ye shall be free indeed.

Psalms 107:14 (New International Version)
He brought them out of darkness, the utter darkness, and broke away their chains.

Psalm 32: 7 (New International Version)
You are my hiding place; you will protect me from trouble and surround me with songs of deliverance.

ACKNOWLEDGEMENTS

Thanks to Chaundivia Richardson, Shirley Banks, Monica Frazier and Vanessa Jones Nwaugo for your support of this project.

AUTHOR BIO

Chaundria R. Zeigler is a Medical Records Associate of 14 years at Roswell Park Cancer Institute in Buffalo, NY. Despite the everyday challenges of being a single mother, in her spare time, she worked hard to become a graduate of the Sound of the Genuine Biblical Institute and is now working towards becoming a licensed minister. She currently serves on the intercessory prayer team, as well as Pastoral Care ministry at Edison Street Community Church under the leadership of Pastor Ted Howard Jr.

In her free time, Chaundria enjoys spending time with family, as well as indulging in her love and passion for travel. Chaundria is the proud mother of 3 girls Chauntavia, Chaundivia and Dejahnique; and 1 son Shawn Jr., along with 4 grandchildren whom she adores.

CONTACT INFORMATION

chaundriazeigler@yahoo.com

chaundriazeiglerministries.com